Pope Francis
and the Family

*All booklets are published thanks to the
generous support of the members of the
Catholic Truth Society*

CATHOLIC TRUTH SOCIETY
PUBLISHERS TO THE HOLY SEE

ISBN 978 1 78469 090 8

CONTENTS

Nazareth

The Synod of Bishops on the Family, recently celebrated, was the first stage of a journey, which will conclude next October with the celebration of another Assembly on the theme: "The Vocation and Mission of the Family in the Church and [Contemporary] World". The prayer and reflection which must accompany this journey is required of all the People of God. I would also like the customary meditations of the Wednesday Audiences to be included in this common journey. I have therefore decided to reflect with you, this year, precisely on the family, on this great gift that the Lord has made to the world from the very beginning, when he entrusted Adam and Eve with the mission to multiply and fill the earth (cf. *Gn* 1:28); that gift that Jesus confirmed and sealed in his Gospel.

The nearness of Christmas casts a great light on this mystery. The Incarnation of the Son of God opens a new beginning in the universal history of man and woman. And this new beginning happens within a family, in Nazareth. Jesus was born in a family. He could have come in a spectacular way, or as a warrior, an emperor…. No, no: he is born in a family, in a family. This is important: to perceive in the Nativity, this beautiful scene.

Dwelling on the periphery

God chose to come into the world in a human family, which he himself formed. He formed it in a remote village on the outskirts of the Roman Empire. Not in Rome, which was the capital of the Empire, not in a big city, but on its nearly invisible outskirts, indeed, of little renown. The Gospels also recall this, almost as an expression: "Can anything good come out of Nazareth?" (*Jn* 1:46). Perhaps, in many parts of the world, we still talk this way, when we hear the name of some areas on the periphery of a big city. And so, right there, on the outskirts of the great Empire, began the most holy and good story of Jesus among men! And that is where this family was.

Jesus dwelt on that periphery for thirty years. The Evangelist Luke summarises this period like this: Jesus "was obedient to them" - that is, to Mary and Joseph. And someone might say: "But did this God, who comes to save us, waste thirty years there, in that suburban slum?" He wasted thirty years! He wanted this. Jesus' path was in that family - "and his mother kept all these things in her heart. And Jesus increased in wisdom and in stature, and in favour with God and man" (*Lk* 2:51-52). It does not recount miracles or healing, or preaching - he did none in that period - or of crowds flocking; in Nazareth everything seemed to happen "normally", according to the customs of a pious and hardworking Israelite family: they worked, the mother cooked, she did all the housework, ironed shirts...all the things mothers do. The father, a carpenter, worked, taught his son the trade. Thirty years. "But what a waste, Father!" God works in mysterious ways. But what was important there was the family! And this was not a waste! They were great Saints: Mary, the most holy woman, immaculate, and Joseph, a most righteous man…. The family.

How much we can learn

We are certainly moved by the story of how the adolescent Jesus followed the religious calendar of the community and the social duties; in knowing how, as a young worker, he worked with Joseph; and then how he attended the reading of the Scriptures, in praying the Psalms and in so many other customs of daily life. The Gospels, in their sobriety, make no reference to Jesus' adolescence and leave this task to our loving meditation. Art, literature, music have taken this journey through imagination. It is certainly not difficult to imagine how much mothers could learn from Mary's care for that Son! And how much fathers could glean from the example of Joseph, a righteous man, who dedicated his life to supporting and protecting the Child and his wife - his family - in difficult times. Not to mention how much children could be encouraged by the adolescent Jesus to understand the necessity and beauty of cultivating their most profound vocation and of dreaming great dreams! In those thirty years, Jesus cultivated his vocation, for which the Father had sent him. And in that time, Jesus never became discouraged, but increased in courage in order to carry his mission forward.

Welcome Jesus

Each Christian family can first of all - as Mary and Joseph did - welcome Jesus, listen to him, speak with him, guard him, protect him, grow with him; and in this way improve the world. Let us make room in our heart and in our day for the Lord. As Mary and Joseph also did, and it was not easy: how many difficulties they had to overcome! They were not a superficial family, they were not an unreal family. The family of Nazareth urges us to rediscover the vocation and mission of the family, of every family. And, what happened in those thirty years in Nazareth, can thus happen to us too: in seeking to make love and not hate normal, making mutual help commonplace, not indifference or enmity. It is no coincidence, then, that "Nazareth" means "She who keeps", as Mary, who - as the Gospel states - "kept all these things in her heart" (cf. *Lk* 2:19, 51). Since then, each time there is a family that keeps this mystery, even if it were on the periphery of the world, the mystery of the Son of God, the mystery of Jesus who comes to save us, the mystery is at work. He comes to save the world. And this is the great mission of the family: to make room for Jesus who is coming, to welcome Jesus in the family, in each member: children, husband, wife, grandparents…. Jesus is there. Welcome him there, in order that he grow spiritually in the family.

THE MOTHER

Today we will reflect on Mother Church. The Church is Mother. Our Holy Mother Church.

In these days the Church's liturgy sets before our eyes the icon of the Virgin Mary, Mother of God. The first day of the year is the Feast of the Mother of God, followed by the Epiphany, commemorating the visit of the Magi. The Evangelist Matthew writes: "going into the house they saw the Child with Mary his mother, and they fell down and worshiped him" (*Mt* 2:11). It is the Mother who, after giving birth to him, presents the Son to the world. She gives us Jesus, she shows us Jesus, she lets us see Jesus.

Let us continue with the catecheses on the family, and in the family there is *the mother*. Every human person owes his or her life to a mother, and almost always owes much of what follows in life, both human and spiritual formation, to her. Yet, despite being highly lauded from a symbolic point of view - many poems, many beautiful things said poetically of her - the mother is rarely listened to or helped in daily life, rarely considered central to society in her role. Rather, often the readiness of mothers to make sacrifices for their children is taken advantage of so as to "save" on social spending.

It also happens that in Christian communities the mother is not always held in the right regard, she is barely heard. Yet the centre of the life of the Church is the Mother of Jesus. Perhaps mothers, ready to sacrifice so much for their children and often for others as well, ought to be listened to more. We should understand more about their daily struggle to be efficient at work and attentive and affectionate in the family; we should better grasp what they aspire to in order to express the best and most authentic fruits of their emancipation. A mother with her children always has problems, always work. I remember there were five of us children at home, and while one was doing one thing, the other wanted to do another, and our poor mama went back and forth from one side to another, but she was happy. She gave us so much.

Martyrdom of motherhood

Mothers are the strongest antidote to the spread of self-centred individualism. "Individual" means "what cannot be divided". Mothers, instead, "divide" themselves, from the moment they bear a child to give him to the world and help him grow. It is they, mothers, who most hate war, which kills their children. Many times I have thought of those mothers who receive the letter: "I inform you that your son has fallen in defence of his homeland…". The poor women! How a mother suffers! It is they who testify to the beauty of life. Archbishop Óscar Arnulfo Romero said that mothers experience a "martyrdom of motherhood". In the homily for the funeral of a priest assassinated by death squads, he said, recalling the Second Vatican Council:

"We must be ready to die for our faith, even if the Lord does not grant us this honour…. Giving one's life does not only mean being killed; giving one's life, having the spirit of a martyr, it is in giving in duty, in silence, in prayer, in honest fulfilment of his duty; in that silence of daily life; giving one's life little by little. Yes, like it is given by a mother, who without fear and with the simplicity of the martyrdom of motherhood, conceives a child in her womb, gives birth to him, nurses him, helps them grow and cares for them with affection. She gives her life. That's martyrdom".

Yes, being a mother doesn't only mean bringing a child to the world, but it is also a life choice. What does a mother choose, what is the life choice of a mother? The life choice of a mother is the choice to give life. And this is great, this is beautiful.

Witnesses of tenderness

A society without mothers would be a dehumanised society, for mothers are always, even in the worst moments, witnesses of tenderness, dedication and moral strength. Mothers often pass on the deepest sense of religious practice: in a human being's life, the value of faith is inscribed in the first prayers, the first acts of devotion that a child learns. It is a message that believing mothers are able to pass on without much explanation: these come later, but the seed of faith is those early precious moments. Without mothers, not only would there be no new faithful, but the faith would lose a good part of its simple and profound warmth. And the Church is Mother, with all of this, she is our mother! We are not orphans, we have a mother! Our Lady, Mother Church, is our mum. We are not orphans, we are children of the Church, we are children of Our Lady, and we are children of our mothers.

Dearest mothers, thank you, thank you for what you are in your family and for what you give to the Church and the world. And to you, beloved Church, thank you, thank you for being Mother. And to you, Mary, Mother of God, thank you for letting us see Jesus.

THE ABSENT FATHER

Now we shall take the word "father" as our guide. It is a term dearer than any other to us Christians because it is the name by which Jesus taught us to call God: father. The meaning of this name took on new depth from the very way Jesus used it to turn to God and to manifest his special relationship with Him. The blessed mystery of God's intimacy, Father, Son and Spirit revealed by Jesus, is the heart of our Christian faith.

"Father" is a term familiar to everyone, a universal word. It indicates a fundamental relationship, the reality of which is as old as human history. Today, however, one has reached the point of claiming that our society is a "society without fathers". In other words, particularly in Western culture, the father figure would be symbolically absent, paled, removed. At first, this was perceived as a liberation: liberation from the father-master, from the father as the representative of the law that is imposed from without, from the father as the censor of his children's happiness and the obstacle to the emancipation and autonomy of young people. At times in some homes authoritarianism reigned in the past, in some cases even oppression: parents who treated their children like servants, not respecting their individual needs for growth; fathers who did not help them to start out on their journey with freedom - and it is not easy to bring up a child in freedom; fathers who did not help them assume their own responsibilities to build their future and that of society.

This, certainly, is not a good approach; but, as often happens, one goes from one extreme to the other. In our day, the problem no longer seems to be the invasive presence of the father so much as his absence, his inaction. Fathers are sometimes so concentrated on themselves and on their work and at times on their career that they even forget about the family. And they leave the little ones and the young ones to themselves. As Bishop of Buenos Aires I sensed the feeling of orphanhood that children are experiencing today, and I often asked fathers if they played with their children, if they had the courage and love to spend time with their kids. And the answer was negative in most cases: "But I can't, because I have so much work...". And the father was absent from the little child growing up, he did not play with him, no, he did not waste time with him.

Shortage of love

Now, on this common journey of reflection on the family, I would like to say to all Christian communities that we must be more attentive: the absent father figure in the life of little ones and young people causes gaps and wounds that may even be very serious. And, in effect, delinquency among children and adolescents can be largely attributed to this lack, to the shortage of examples and authoritative guidance in their everyday life, a shortage of closeness, a shortage of love from the father. And the feeling of orphanhood that so many young people live with is more profound than we think.

They are orphaned in the family, because the father is often absent, also physically, from the home, but above all because, when they are present, they do not behave like fathers. They do not converse with their children. They do not fulfil their role as educators. They do not set their children a good example with their words, principles, values, those rules of life which they need like bread. The educative quality of the time the father spends raising the child is all the more necessary when he is forced to stay away from home because of work. Sometimes it seems that fathers don't know what their role in the family is or how to raise their children. So, in doubt, they abstain, they retreat and neglect their responsibilities, perhaps taking refuge in the unlikely relationship as "equals" with their children. It's true that you have to be a "companion" to your child, but without forgetting that you are the father! If you behave only as a peer to your child, it will do him or her no good.

Paternal responsibility

We also see this problem in the civil community. The civil community with its institutions, has a certain - let's call it paternal - responsibility towards young people, a responsibility that at times is neglected or poorly exercised. It too often leaves them orphaned and does not offer them a true perspective. Young people are thus deprived of safe paths to follow, of teachers to trust in, of ideals to warm their hearts, of values and of hopes to sustain them daily. They become filled perhaps with idols, but their hearts are robbed; they are obliged to dream of amusement and pleasure, but they are not given work; they become deluded by the god of money, and they are denied true wealth.

And so it would do everyone good, fathers and children, to listen again to the promise that Jesus made to his disciples: "I will not leave you orphans" (cf. *Jn* 14:18). He is, indeed, the Way to follow, the Teacher to listen to, the Hope that the world can change, that love conquers hatred, that there can be a future of brotherhood and peace for all. One of you might say to me: "But Father, today you were too negative. You only spoke about the absent father, what happens when fathers are not close to their children…" It's true, I wanted to stress this, because next Wednesday I am going to continue this catechesis by highlighting the beauty of fatherhood. That is why I chose to start from the darkness, in order to reach the light. May the Lord help us understand these things better.

THE FATHER WHO IS PRESENT

I would like to develop the second part of my reflection on the figure of the father in the family. Last time I spoke about the danger of "absent" fathers, now I would like to look instead at the positive aspect. Even St Joseph was tempted to leave Mary, when he discovered that she was pregnant; but the Angel of the Lord intervened and revealed to him God's plan and his mission as foster father; and Joseph, a just man, "took his wife" (*Mt* 1:24) and became the father of the family of Nazareth.

Every family needs a father. We shall reflect on the value of his role, and I would like to begin with a few expressions that we find in the Book of Proverbs, words that a father addresses to his own son, and it reads like this: "My son, if your heart is wise, my heart too will be glad. My soul will rejoice when your lips speak what is right" (*Pr* 23:15-16). Nothing could better express the pride and emotion a father feels when he understands that he has handed down to his child what really matters in life, that is, a wise heart. This father does not say: "I am proud of you because you are the same as me, because you repeat the things I say and do." No, he does not say anything so simple to him. He says something much more important, which we can understand in this way: "I will be happy every time I see you act with wisdom, and I will be moved every time that I hear you speak with rectitude. This is what I wanted to leave to you, that this one thing become yours: the attitude to feel and act, to speak and judge with wisdom and rectitude. And that you might be like this, I taught you the things you didn't know, I corrected the errors you didn't see. I made you feel a profound and at the same time discrete affection, which maybe you did not fully recognise when you were young and unsure. I gave you a testimony of rigour and steadfastness that perhaps you didn't understand, when you would have liked only complicity and protection. I had first to test myself in the wisdom of my heart, be vigilant of my excesses of sentiment and resentment, in order to carry the weight of the inevitable misunderstandings, to find the right words to make myself understood." "Now," continues the father, "I see that you strive to be this way with your own children, and with everyone, and it moves me. I am happy to be your father." This is what a wise father, a mature father, says. A father knows all too well what it costs to hand down this heritage: how close, how gentle and how firm to be. But what consolation and what recompense he receives when the children honour this legacy! It is a joy that rewards all the toil, that overcomes every misunderstanding and heals every wound.

Be present, not controlling

The first need, then, is precisely this: that a father be *present* in the family. That he be close to his wife, to share everything, joy and sorrow, hope and hardship. And that he be close to his children as they grow: when they play and when they strive, when they are carefree and when they are distressed, when they are talkative and when they are silent, when they are daring and when they are afraid, when they take a wrong step and when they find their path again; a father who is always present. To say "present" is not to say "controlling"! Fathers who are too controlling cancel out their children, they don't let them develop.

The Gospel speaks to us about the exemplarity of the Father who is in heaven - who alone, Jesus says, can be truly called the "good Father" (cf. *Mk* 10:18). Everyone knows that extraordinary parable of the "prodigal son", or better yet of the "merciful father", which we find in the Gospel of Luke in chapter 15 (cf. 15:11-32). What dignity and what tenderness there is in the expectation of that father, who stands at the door of the house waiting for his son to return! Fathers must be patient. Often there is nothing else to do but wait; pray and wait with patience, gentleness, magnanimity and mercy.

The good father knows how to wait

A good father *knows how to wait and knows how to forgive* from the depths of his heart. Certainly, he also knows how to correct with firmness: he is not a weak father, submissive and sentimental. The father who *knows how to correct without humiliating* is the one who knows how to protect without sparing himself. Once I heard a father at a meeting on marriage say: "Sometimes I have to strike the children lightly... but never in the face so as not to humiliate them." How beautiful! He has a sense of dignity. He must punish, but he does it in a just way, and moves on.

If, then, there is someone who can fully explain the prayer of the "Our Father", taught by Jesus, it is the one who lives out paternity in the first person. Without the grace that comes from the Father who is in heaven, fathers lose courage, and abandon camp. But children need to find a father waiting for them when they come home after failing. They will do everything not to admit it, not to show it, but they need it; and not to find it opens wounds in them that are difficult to heal.

The Church, our mother, is committed to supporting with all her strength the good and generous presence of fathers in families, for they are the irreplaceable guardians and mediators of faith in goodness, of faith in justice and in God's protection, like St Joseph.

THE CHILDREN

After reflecting on the figures of the mother and father, in this catechesis on the family I would like to talk about the child, or even better, about children. I shall use a beautiful image from Isaiah. The Prophet writes: "they all gather together, they come to you; your sons shall come from far, and your daughters shall be carried in the arms. Then you shall see and be radiant, your heart shall thrill and rejoice" (60:4-5). It is a splendid image, an image of happiness which is fulfilled in the reunion of parents and children, who journey together toward a future of freedom and peace, after a long period of deprivation and separation, when the Hebrew people were far from their homeland.

In essence, there is a close link between the hope of a people and the harmony among generations. We must consider this carefully. There is a close link between the hope of a people and the harmony among generations. The joy of children causes the parents' hearts to beat and reopens the future. Children are the joy of the family and of society. They are not a question of reproductive biology, nor one of the many ways to fulfil oneself, much less a possession of their parents.... No. Children are a gift, they are a gift: understood? Children are a gift. Each one is unique and irreplaceable; and at the same time unmistakably linked to his or her roots. In fact, according to God's plan, being son and daughter means to carry within oneself the memory and hope of a love which was fulfilled in the very kindling of the life of another, original and new, human being. And for parents each child is original, different, diverse. Allow me to share a family memory. I remember what my mother said about us - there were five of us: - "I have five children." When they asked her: "Which one is your favourite?" she answered: "I have five children, like five fingers. [He displays his fingers.] Should they strike this one, it hurts me; should they strike that one, it hurts me. All five hurt me. All are my children and all are different like the fingers of a hand." And this is how a family is! The children are all different, but all children.

A child is a child!

A child is loved because he is one's child: not because he is beautiful, or because he is like this or like that; no, because he is a child! Not because he thinks as I do, or embodies my dreams. A child is a child: a life generated by us but intended for him, for his good, for the good of the family, of society, of mankind as a whole.

From this also derives the depth of the human experience of being son or daughter, which allows us to discover the most gratuitous dimension of love, which never ceases to astonish us. It is the beauty of being loved first: children are loved before they arrive. So often I find mothers in the Square who are expecting a baby and ask me for a blessing…these babies are loved before coming into the world. And this is free, this is love; they are loved before being born, like the love of God who always loves us first. They are loved before having done anything to deserve it, before knowing how to talk or think, even before coming into the world! Being children is the basic condition for knowing the love of God, which is the ultimate source of this authentic miracle. In the soul of every child, inasmuch as it is vulnerable, God places the seal of this love, which is at the basis of his or her personal dignity, a dignity which nothing and no one can ever destroy.

Building a new world

Today it seems more difficult for children to imagine their future. Fathers - I touched on this in previous catecheses - have perhaps taken a step backwards and children have become more uncertain in taking their steps forward. We can learn the good relationship between generations from our Heavenly Father, who leaves each of us free, but never leaves us on our own. And if we err, He continues to follow us with patience, without abating his love for us. Our Heavenly Father does not take steps back in his love for us, ever! He always goes forwards and if he cannot go forwards he waits for us, but he never goes backwards; he wants his children to be brave and take their steps forward.

The children, for their part, must not be afraid of the task of building a new world: it is right for them to want to improve on what they have received! But this must be done without arrogance, without presumption. One must know how to recognise a child's virtue, and parents always deserve honour.

We are all children

The fourth Commandment asks children - we are all children! - to honour our father and mother (cf. *Ex* 20:12). This Commandment comes immediately after those regarding God Himself. Indeed, it contains something sacred, something divine, something which lies at the root of every other type of respect among men. And to the biblical formulation of the fourth Commandment is added: "that your days may be long in the land which the Lord your God gives you". The virtuous bond between generations is the guarantee of the future, and is the guarantee of a truly human history. A society with children who do not honour parents is a society without honour; when one does not honour one's parents one loses one's own honour! It is a society destined to be filled with arid and greedy young people. However, even a society with a paucity of generations, which does not love being surrounded by children, which considers them above all a worry, a weight, a risk, is a depressed society. Let us consider the many societies we know here in Europe:

they are depressed societies, because they do not want children, they are not having children, the birth rate does not reach one percent. Why? Let each of us consider and respond. If a family with many children is looked upon as a burden, something is wrong! The child's generation must be responsible, as the Encyclical *Humanae Vitae* of Blessed Pope Paul VI also teaches, but having many children cannot automatically be an irresponsible choice. Not to have children is a selfish choice. Life is rejuvenated and acquires energy by multiplying: it is enriched, not impoverished! Children learn to assume responsibility for their family. They mature in sharing its hardship. They grow in the appreciation of its gifts. The happy experience of brotherhood inspires respect and care for parents, to whom our recognition is due. So many of you present here have children and we are all children. Let us do something, let us observe a moment of silence. Each of us think in our heart about our children - if we have any - think in silence. And let us all think about our parents and thank God for the gift of life. In silence, those who have children think of them, and everyone think of our parents.

May the Lord bless our parents and bless your children. May Jesus, the eternal Son, who in the fullness of time became a child, help us find the path of a new radiation of this so great and so simple human experience of being children. In the multiplication of generations there is a mystery of enrichment of the life of all, which comes from God Himself. We must rediscover it, challenging prejudice; and live it, in the faith, in perfect happiness.

BROTHERS AND SISTERS

Having considered the roles of the mother, the father, the children, we shall reflect on *siblings*. "Brother" and "sister" are words that Christianity really loves. And, thanks to the family experience, they are words that all cultures and all times comprehend.

The fraternal bond holds a special place *in the history of the People of God*, who received his revelation at the core of the human experience. The Psalmist sings of the beauty of the fraternal bond: "Behold, how good and pleasant it is when brothers dwell in unity!" (*Ps* 133[132]:1). And this is true, brotherhood is beautiful! Jesus Christ also brought to its fullness this human experience of being brothers and sisters, embracing it in Trinitarian love and thereby empowering it to go well beyond the ties of kinship and enabling it to surmount every barrier of extraneousness.

We know that *when the fraternal relationship is destroyed*, when the relationship between siblings is destroyed, the road is open to painful experiences of conflict, of betrayal, of hate. The biblical account of *Cain and Abel* is an example of this negative outcome. After the killing of Abel, God asks Cain: "Where is Abel your brother?" (*Gn* 4:9a). It is a question that the Lord continues to repeat to every generation. And unfortunately, in every generation, Cain's dramatic answer never fails to be repeated: "I do not know; am I my brother's keeper?" (*ibid.*, 4:9b). The rupture of the bond between siblings is a nasty, bad thing for humanity. In the family too, how many siblings quarrel over little things, or over an inheritance, and then they no longer speak to each other, they no longer greet one another. This is terrible! Brotherhood is a great thing, when we consider that all our brothers and sisters lived in the womb of the same mother for nine months, came from the mother's flesh! Brotherhood cannot be broken. Let us consider: we all know families that have divided siblings, who have quarrelled; let us ask the Lord - perhaps in our family there are a few cases - to help these families to reunite their siblings, to rebuild the family. Brotherhood must not be broken and when it breaks, what happened to Cain and Abel occurs. When the Lord asks Cain where his brother is, he replies: "I do not know, my brother does not matter to me." This is terrible, it is a very, very painful thing to hear. In our prayers let us always pray for siblings who are at odds.

Nourished by affection

Should the bond of *fraternity* which *forms in the family between children* arise in an educational atmosphere of openness to others, it is the great school of freedom and peace. In the family, among siblings, human co-existence is learned, how one must live in society. Perhaps we are not always aware of it, but the family itself introduces fraternity into the world! Beginning with this first experience of fraternity, nourished by affection and education at home, the style of fraternity radiates like a promise upon the whole of society and on its relations among peoples.

The blessing that God, *in Jesus Christ*, pours out on this bond of fraternity, *expands* in an unimaginable way. He renders it capable of overcoming all differences of nationality, language, culture and even religion.

Consider what becomes of the bond between men and women, even when completely different from each other, when they are able to say of another: "He is truly like a brother, she is just like a sister to me!" This is beautiful! History has shown well enough, after all, that even freedom and equality, without brotherhood, can be full of individualism and conformism, and even personal interests.

Familial fraternity shines in a special way when we see the care, the patience, the affection that envelop *the weakest little brother or sister*, sick or physically challenged. There are countless brothers and sisters who do this, throughout the world, and perhaps we do not appreciate their generosity enough. And when there are many siblings in a family - today, I greeted a family that has nine children - the eldest boy or girl helps the dad, the mum, to take care of the younger children. This work of helping among siblings is beautiful.

Christian fraternity

Having a brother, a sister, who loves you is a deep, precious, irreplaceable experience. *Christian fraternity* happens in the same way. The smallest, the weakest, the poorest soften us: they have the "right" to take our heart and soul. Yes, they are our brothers and sisters and as such we must love and care for them. When this happens, when the poor are like family members, our own Christian fraternity comes to life again. Christians, in fact, go to meet the poor and the weak not to obey an ideological programme, but because the word and the example of the Lord tell us that we are all brothers and sisters. This is the principle of God's love and of all justice among men. I should like to suggest something: before concluding, just a few words, in silence each of us, let us think of our brothers, our sisters, and from our heart let us pray in silence for them. A moment of silence.

Here then, with this prayer we have brought all, brothers and sisters, with our thoughts, with our hearts, here to the Square to receive the blessing.

Today more than ever it is necessary to place fraternity back at the centre of our technocratic and bureaucratic society: then even freedom and equality will find the correct balance. Therefore, let us not thoughtlessly deprive our families, out of criticism or fear, of the beauty of a bountiful fraternal experience of sons and daughters. And let us not lose our trust in the broad horizon faith is able to draw from this experience, enlightened by God's blessing.

THE ELDERLY

This catechesis and the next will be dedicated to the elderly, who in the family are the *grandparents, aunts and uncles*. We will reflect on the current problematic condition of the elderly, and next time, that is, next Wednesday, on a more positive note, on the vocation pertaining to this stage of life.

Thanks to the progress of medicine lifespans have increased: but society *has not "expanded" to life*! The number of elderly has multiplied, but our societies are not organised well enough to make room for them, with proper respect and practical consideration for their frailty and their dignity. While we are young, we are led to ignore old age, as if it were a disease to keep away from; then when we become old, especially if we are poor, if we are sick and alone, we experience the shortcomings of a society programmed for efficiency, which consequently ignores its elderly. And the elderly are a wealth not to be ignored.

Benedict XVI, visiting a home for the elderly, used clear and prophetic words, saying in this way: "The quality of a society, I mean of a civilisation, is also judged by how it treats elderly people and by the place it gives them in community life" (12th November 2012). It's true, attention to the elderly makes the difference in a civilisation. Is there attention to the elderly in a civilisation? Is there room for the elderly? This civilisation will move forward if it knows how to respect wisdom, the wisdom of the elderly. In a civilisation in which there is no room for the elderly or where they are thrown away because they create problems, this society carries with it the virus of death.

Throw-away culture

In the West, scientists present the current century as *the aging century*: children are diminishing, the elderly are increasing. This imbalance challenges us, indeed, it is a great challenge for contemporary society. Yet a culture of profit insists on casting off the old like a "weight". Not only do they not produce - this culture thinks - but they are a burden: in short, what is the outcome of thinking like this? They are thrown away. It's brutal to see how the elderly are thrown away, it is a brutal thing, it is a sin! No one dares to say it openly, but it's done! There is something vile in this *adherence to the throw-away culture*. But we are accustomed to throwing people away. We want to remove our growing fear of weakness and vulnerability; but by doing so we increase in the elderly the anxiety of being poorly tolerated and neglected.

During my ministry in Buenos Aires I was in direct contact with this reality and its problems:

"The elderly are abandoned, and not only in material instability. They are abandoned out of a selfish incapacity to accept their limitations that reflect our own limitations, because of the numerous difficulties that must be overcome in order to survive in a society that does not allow them to participate, to have their say, or be referents in the consumer model of 'only the young can be useful and enjoy'. These elderly persons throughout society ought to be a reservoir of wisdom for our people. The elderly are the reservoir of wisdom for our people! How easily the conscience falls dormant when there is no love!" (*Solo l'amore ci può salvare*, Vatican City, 2013, p. 83).

And it happens like that. I remember, when I was visiting a retirement home, I spoke with each person and I frequently heard this: "How are you?" - "And your children?" - "Well, well." - "How many do you have?" - "Many." - "And do they come to visit you?" - "Oh sure, yes, always, yes, they come." "When was the last time they came?" I remember an elderly woman who said to me: "Mmm, for Christmas." It was August! Eight months without being visited by her children, abandoned for eight months! This is called mortal sin, understand? Once as a child, a grandmother told us the story of an old grandfather who got dirty while eating because he couldn't easily bring the spoonful of soup to his mouth. And his son, that is, the father of the family, had decided to move him from the dinner table and set up a little table in the kitchen to eat alone, so he couldn't be seen. In this way he wouldn't make a bad impression when friends came over to lunch or dinner. A few days later, he came home and found his youngest child playing with some wood and a hammer and nails, he was making something there, he said: "What are you making?" - "I'm making a table, papa." - "A table, why?" - "To have one for when you grow old, so that you can eat there". Children are more aware than we are!

Wisdom of the elderly

In the tradition of the Church there is a *wealth of wisdom* that has always supported a culture of *closeness to the elderly*, a disposition of warm and supportive companionship in this final phase of life. This tradition is rooted in Sacred Scripture, as these passages from the Book of Sirach attest: "Do not disregard the discourse of the aged, for they themselves learned from their fathers; because from them you will gain understanding and learn how to give an answer in time of need" (*Sir* 8:9).

The Church cannot and does not want to conform to a mentality of impatience, and much less of indifference and contempt, towards old age. We must reawaken the *collective sense of gratitude*, of appreciation, of hospitality, which makes the elder feel like a living part of his community.

Our elders are men and women, fathers and mothers,

who came before us on our own road, in our own house, in our daily battle for a worthy life. They are men and women from whom we have received so much. The elder is not an alien. We are that elder: in the near or far future, but inevitably, even if we don't think it. And if we don't learn how to treat the elder better, that is how we will be treated.

We old people are all a little fragile. Some, however, are *particularly weak*, many are alone, and stricken by illness. Some depend on the indispensable care and attention of others. Are we going to take a step back? Abandon them to their fate? A society without *proximity*, where *gratuity* and affection *without compensation* - between strangers as well - is disappearing, is a perverse society. The Church, faithful to the Word of God, cannot tolerate such degeneration. A Christian community in which proximity and gratuity are no longer considered indispensable is a society which would lose her soul. Where there is no honour for elders, there is no future for the young.

The Grandparents

We continue our reflection on grandparents, *considering the value and importance of their role in the family*. I do so by placing myself in their shoes, because I too belong to this age group.

When I was in the Philippines, the Filipino people greeted me saying: "Lolo Kiko" - meaning Grandpa Francis - "Lolo Kiko", they said! The first important thing to stress: it is true that society tends to discard us, but the Lord definitely does not! The Lord never discards us. He calls us to follow Him in every age of life, and *old age has a grace and a mission* too, a true vocation from the Lord. Old age is a vocation. It is not yet time to "pull in the oars". This period of life is different from those before, there is no doubt; we even have to somewhat "invent it ourselves", because our societies are not ready, spiritually and morally, to appreciate the true value of this stage of life. Indeed, it once was not so normal to have time available; it is much more so today. Christian spirituality has also been caught somewhat by surprise, with regard to outlining a kind of spirituality of the elderly. But thanks be to God there is no shortage of the testimony of elderly saints, both men and women!

Simeon and Anna

I was really moved by the "Day Dedicated to the Elderly" that we had here in St Peter's Square last year, the Square was full. I listened to the stories of elderly people who devote themselves to others, and to stories of married couples, who said: "We are celebrating our fiftieth wedding anniversary, we are celebrating our sixtieth wedding anniversary." It is important to present this to young people who tire so easily; the testimony of the elderly in fidelity is important. There were so many in this Square that day. It is a reflection to continue, in both the ecclesial and civil spheres. The Gospel comes to meet us with a really moving and encouraging image. It is the image of Simeon and Anna, whom are spoken of in the Gospel of Jesus' childhood, composed by St Luke. There were certainly elderly, the "old man", Simeon, and the "prophetess", Anna, who was eighty four years old. This woman did not hide her age. The Gospel says that they awaited the coming of God every day, with great trust, for many years. They truly wanted to see Him that day, to grasp the signs, to understand the origin. By then, they were also perhaps more resigned to die first: that long wait, however, continued to occupy their whole life, having no commitments more important than this: to await the Lord and pray. So, when Mary and Joseph went to the temple to fulfil the provisions of the Law, Simeon and Anna moved quickly, inspired by the Holy Spirit (cf. *Lk* 2:27).

The burden of age and waiting disappeared in an instant. They recognised the Child, and discovered *new strength, for a new task*: to give thanks for and bear witness to this Sign from God. Simeon improvised a beautiful hymn of jubilation (cf. *Lk* 2:29-32) - in that moment he was a poet - and Anna became the first woman to preach of Jesus: she "spoke of him to all who were looking for the redemption of Jerusalem" (*Lk* 2:38).

Prayer is a great gift

Dear grandparents, dear elderly, let us follow in the footsteps of these extraordinary elders! Let us too become like poets of prayer: let us develop a taste for finding our own words, let us once again grasp those which teach us the Word of God. *The prayer of grandparents and of the elderly is a great gift for the Church!* The prayer of grandparents and of the elderly is a great gift for the Church, it is a treasure! A great injection of wisdom for the whole of human society: above all for one which is too busy, too taken, too distracted. Someone should also sing, for them too, sing of the signs of God, proclaim the signs of God, pray for them! Let us look to Benedict XVI, who chose to spend the final span of his life in prayer and listening to God! This is beautiful! A great believer of the last century, of the Orthodox tradition, Olivier Clément, said: "A civilisation which has no place for prayer is a civilisation in which old age has lost all meaning. And this is terrifying. For, above all, we need old people who pray; prayer is the purpose of old age". We need old people who pray because this is the very purpose of old age. The prayer of the elderly is a beautiful thing.

We are able to *thank* the Lord for the benefits received, and fill the emptiness of ingratitude that surrounds us. We are able to *intercede* for the expectations of younger generations and give dignity to the memory and sacrifices of past generations. We are able to remind ambitious young people that a life without love is a barren life. We are able say to young people who are afraid that anxiety about the future can be overcome. We are able to teach the young who are overly self-absorbed that there is more joy in giving than in receiving. Grandfathers and grandmothers form the enduring "chorus" of a great spiritual sanctuary, where prayers of supplication and songs of praise sustain the community which toils and struggles in the field of life.

Encourage the young

Last, prayer *unceasingly purifies the heart*. Praise and supplication to God prevents the heart from becoming hardened by resentment and selfishness. How awful is the cynicism of an elderly person who has lost the meaning of his testimony, who scorns the young and does not communicate the wisdom of life! How beautiful, however, is the encouragement an elderly person manages to pass onto a young person who is seeking the meaning of faith and of life! It is truly the mission of grandparents, the vocation of the elderly. The words of grandparents have special value for the young. And the young know it. I still carry with me, always, in my breviary, the words my grandmother consigned to me in writing on the day of my priestly ordination. I read them often and they do me good.

How I would like a Church that challenges the throw-away culture with the overflowing joy of a new embrace between young and old! This is what I ask of the Lord today, this embrace!

THE GIFT OF CHILDREN

After reviewing the various members of the family - mother, father, children, siblings, grandparents - I would like to conclude this first group of catecheses on the family by speaking about children. I will do so in two phases: first, I will focus on the great gift that children are for humanity - it is true they are a great gift for humanity, but also really excluded because they are not even allowed to be born - and the next time I shall focus on several wounds that unfortunately harm childhood. Who come to mind are the many children I met during my recent journey to Asia: full of life, of enthusiasm, and, on the other hand, I see that in the world, many of them live in unworthy conditions.... In fact, from the way children are treated society can be judged, not only morally but also sociologically, whether it is a liberal society or a society enslaved by international interests.

First of all children remind us that we all, in the first years of life, were completely dependent upon the care and benevolence of others. The Son of God was not spared this stage. It is the mystery that we contemplate every year at Christmas. The Nativity Scene is the icon which communicates this reality in the simplest and most direct way. It is curious: God has no difficulty in making himself understood by children, and children have no difficulty in understanding God. It is not by chance that in the Gospel there are several very beautiful and powerful words of Jesus regarding the "little ones". This term, "babes", refers to all the people who depend on the help of others, and to children in particular. For example, Jesus says: "I thank thee, Father, Lord of heaven and earth, that thou hast hidden these things from the wise and understanding, and revealed them to babes" (*Mt* 11:25). And again: "See that you do not despise one of these little ones: for I tell you that in heaven their angels always behold the face of my Father who is in heaven" (*Mt* 18:10).

Always sons and daughters

Thus, children are in and of themselves a treasure for humanity and also for the Church, for they constantly evoke that necessary condition for entering the Kingdom of God: that of not considering ourselves self-sufficient, but in need of help, of love, of forgiveness. We all are in need of help, of love and of forgiveness! Children remind us of another beautiful thing: they remind us that we are always sons and daughters. Even if one becomes an adult, or an elder, even if one becomes a parent, if one occupies a position of responsibility, underneath all of this is still the identity of a child. We are all sons and daughters. And this always brings us back to the fact that we did not give ourselves life, but that we received it. The great gift of life is the first gift that we received. Sometimes in life we risk forgetting about this, as if we were the masters of our existence, and instead we are fundamentally dependent. In reality, it is a motive of great joy to feel at every stage of life, in every situation, in every social condition, that we are and we remain sons and daughters. This is the main message that children give us, by their very presence: simply by their presence they remind us that each and every one of us is a son or daughter.

But there are so many gifts, so many riches that children bring to humanity. I shall mention only a few.

They bring their way of seeing reality, with a trusting and pure gaze. A child has spontaneous trust in his father and mother; he has spontaneous trust in God, in Jesus, in Our Lady. At the same time, his interior gaze is pure, not yet tainted by malice, by duplicity, by the "incrustations" of life which harden the heart. We know that children are also marked by original sin, that they are selfish, but they preserve purity, and interior simplicity. But children are not diplomats: they say what they feel, say what they see, directly. And so often they put their parents in difficulty, saying in front of other people: "I don't like this because it is ugly," But children say what they see, they are not two-faced, they have not yet learned that science of duplicity that we adults have unfortunately learned.

Simplicity and tenderness

Furthermore, children - in their interior simplicity - bring with them the capacity to receive and give tenderness.

Tenderness is having a heart "of flesh" and not "of stone", as the Bible says (cf. *Ez* 36:26). Tenderness is also poetry: it is "feeling" things and events, not treating them as mere objects, only to use them, because they are useful....

Children have the capacity to smile and to cry. Some, when I pick them up to embrace them, smile; others see me dressed in white and think I am a doctor and that I am going to vaccinate them, and they cry...spontaneously! Children are like this: they smile and cry, two things which are often "stifled" in grown-ups, we are no longer capable.... So often our smile becomes a cardboard smile, fixed, a smile that is not natural, even an artificial smile, like a clown. Children smile spontaneously and cry spontaneously. It always depends on the heart, and often our heart is blocked and loses this capacity to smile, to cry. So children can teach us how to smile and cry again. But we must ask ourselves: do I smile spontaneously, frankly, with love or is my smile artificial? Do I still cry or have I lost the capacity to cry? These are two very human questions that children teach us.

For all these reasons Jesus invited his disciples to "become like children", because "the Kingdom of God belongs to those who are like them" (cf. *Mt* 18:3; *Mk* 10:14).

Dear brothers and sisters, children bring life, cheerfulness, hope, also troubles. But such is life. Certainly, they also bring worries and sometimes many problems; but better a society with these worries and these problems, than a sad, grey society because it is without children! When we see that the birth rate of a society is barely one percent, we can say that this society is sad, it is grey because it has no children.

THE SUFFERINGS OF CHILDREN

In this series of Catecheses on the family, we are completing our reflection on children, who are the most beautiful gift and blessing that the Creator has given to man and woman. We have already spoken about the great gift that children are. In this catechesis sadly we must speak about the "passions" which many of them endure.

From the first moments of their lives, many children are rejected, abandoned and robbed of their childhood and future. There are those who dare to say, as if to justify themselves, that it was a mistake to bring these children into the world. This is shameful! Let's not unload our faults onto the children, please! Children are never a "mistake". Their hunger is not a mistake, nor is their poverty, their vulnerability, their abandonment - so many children abandoned on the streets - and neither is their ignorance or their helplessness... so many children don't even know what a school is. If anything, these should be reasons to love them all the more, with greater generosity. How can we make such solemn declarations on human rights and the rights of children, if we then punish children for the errors of adults?

We are responsible for children

Those who have the task of governing, of educating, but

I would say all adults, we are responsible for children and for doing what we can to change this situation. I am referring to "the passion" of children. Every child who is marginalised, abandoned, who lives on the street begging with every kind of trick, without schooling, without medical care, is a cry that rises up to God and denounces the system that we adults have set in place. And unfortunately these children are prey to criminals who exploit them for shameful trafficking or commerce, or train them for war and violence. But even in so-called wealthy countries many children live in dramatic situations that scar them deeply because of crises in the family, educational gaps and at times inhuman living conditions. In every case, their childhood is violated in body and soul. But none of these children are forgotten by the Father who is in heaven! Not one of their tears is lost! Neither is our responsibility lost, the social responsibility of people, of each one of us, and of countries.

Once Jesus rebuked his disciples because they sent away the children whose parents brought them to Him to be blessed. It is a moving Gospel narrative: "Then children were brought to him that he might lay his hands on them and pray. The disciples rebuked the people; but Jesus said: 'Let the children come to me, and do not hinder them; for to such belongs the kingdom of heaven.' And he laid his hands on them and went away" (*Mt* 19:13-15). How beautiful is this trust of the parents and Jesus' response! How I would like this passage to become the norm for all children! It is true that by the grace of God children in grave difficulty are often given extraordinary parents, ready and willing to make every sacrifice. But these parents should not be left alone! We should accompany them in their toil, and also offer them moments of shared joy and light-hearted cheer, so that they are not left with only routine therapy.

What will the children's guardian angels tell God about us?

When it comes to children, no matter what, there should be no utterance of those legal defence-like formulae: "after all, we are not a charity," or, "in private, everyone is free to do as he or she wishes," or even, "we're sorry, but we can't do anything." These words do not count when it comes to children.

Too often the effects of a life worn down by precarious and underpaid work, unsustainable hours, bad transport rebound on the children…. Children also pay the price for immature unions and irresponsible separations: they are the first victims; they suffer the outcome of a culture of exaggerated individual rights, and then the children become more precocious. They often absorb the violence they are not able to "ward off" and before the very eyes of adults are forced to grow accustomed to degradation.

Also in our age, as in the past, the Church sets her motherhood at the service of children and their families.

To parents and children of this world of ours, she bears the blessing of God, motherly tenderness, a firm reproach and strong condemnation. Children are no laughing matter!

Think what a society would be like if it decided, once and for all, to establish this principle: "It's true, we are not perfect and we make many mistakes. But when it comes to the children who come into the world, no sacrifice on the part of adults is too costly or too great, to ensure that no child believe he or she was a mistake, is worthless or is abandoned to a life of wounds and to the arrogance of men." How beautiful a society like this would be! I say that for such a society, much could be forgiven, innumerable errors. Truly a great deal.

The Lord judges our life according to what the angels of children tell him, angels who "always behold the face of the Father who is in heaven" (cf. *Mt* 18:10). Let us always ask ourselves: what will the children's guardian angels tell God about us?

THE CREATION OF MAN AND WOMAN

This catechesis is dedicated to an aspect central to the theme of the family: the great gift that God gave to humanity with the creation of man and woman and with the Sacrament of Marriage. This catechesis and the next one will treat the difference and complementarity between man and woman, who stand at the summit of divine creation; then the two after that will be on other topics concerning marriage.

Let us begin with a brief comment on the first narrative of creation, in the Book of Genesis. Here we read that God, after having created the universe and all living beings, created his masterpiece, the human being, whom He made in his own image: "in the image of God he created them; male and female he created them" (*Gn* 1:27), so says the Book of Genesis.

And as we all know, sexual difference is present in so many forms of life, on the great scale of living beings. But man and woman alone are made in the image and likeness of God: the biblical text repeats it three times in two passages (26-27): man and woman are the image and likeness of God. This tells us that it is not man alone who is the image of God or woman alone who is the image of God, but man and woman as a couple who are the image of

God. The difference between man and woman is not meant to stand in opposition, or to subordinate, but is for the sake of communion and generation, always in the image and likeness of God.

We risk taking a step backwards

Experience teaches us: in order to know oneself well and develop harmoniously, a human being needs the reciprocity of man and woman. When that is lacking, one can see the consequences. We are made to listen to one another and help one another. We can say that without the mutual enrichment of this relationship - in thought and in action, in affection and in work, as well as in faith - the two cannot even understand the depth of what it means to be man and woman.

Modern contemporary culture has opened new spaces, new forms of freedom and new depths in order to enrich the understanding of this difference. But it has also introduced many doubts and much scepticism. For example, I ask myself, if the so-called gender theory is not, at the same time, an expression of frustration and resignation, which seeks to cancel out sexual difference because it no longer knows how to confront it. Yes, we risk taking a step backwards. The removal of difference in fact creates a problem, not a solution. In order to resolve the problems in their relationships, men and women need to speak to one another more, listen to each other more, get to know one another better, love one another more. They must treat each other with respect and co-operate in friendship. On this human basis, sustained by the grace of God, it is possible to plan a lifelong marital and familial union. The marital and familial bond is a serious matter, and it is so for everyone not just for believers. I would urge intellectuals not to leave this theme aside, as if it had to become secondary in order to foster a more free and just society.

What feminine genius can give us

God entrusted the earth to the alliance between man and woman: its failure deprives the earth of warmth and darkens the sky of hope. The signs are already worrisome, and we see them. I would like to indicate, among many others, two points that I believe call for urgent attention.

The first. There is no doubt that we must do far more to advance women, if we want to give more strength to the reciprocity between man and woman. In fact, it is necessary that woman not only be listened to more, but that her voice carry real weight, a recognised authority in society and in the Church. The very way Jesus considered women in a context less favourable than ours, because women in those times were relegated to second place. Jesus considered her in a way which gives off a powerful light, which enlightens a path that leads afar, of which we have only covered a small stretch. We have not yet understood in depth what the feminine genius can give us, what woman can give to society and also to us. Maybe women see things in a way that complements the thoughts of men. It is a path to follow with greater creativity and courage.

Crisis of collective trust in God

A second reflection concerns the topic of man and woman created in the image of God. I wonder if the crisis of collective trust in God, which does us so much harm, and makes us pale with resignation, incredulity and cynicism, is not also connected to the crisis of the alliance between man and woman. In fact the biblical account, with the great symbolic fresco depicting the earthly paradise and original sin, tells us in fact that the communion with God is reflected in the communion of the human couple and the loss of trust in the Heavenly Father generates division and conflict between man and woman.

The great responsibility of the Church, of all believers, and first of all of believing families, which derives from us, impels people to rediscover the beauty of the creative design that also inscribes the image of God in the alliance between man and woman. The earth is filled with harmony and trust when the alliance between man and woman is lived properly. And if man and woman seek it together, between themselves, and with God, without a doubt they will find it. Jesus encourages us explicitly to bear witness to this beauty, which is the image of God.

In His Own Image

In the preceding catechesis on the family, I meditated on the first narrative of the creation of the human being, in the first chapter of Genesis, where it is written: "God created man in his own image, in the image of God he created him; male and female he created them" (1:27).

I would like to complete the reflection with the second narrative, which we find in the second chapter. Here we read that the Lord, after having created heaven and earth, "formed man of dust from the ground, and breathed into his nostrils the breath of life; and man became a living being" (2:7). This is the culmination of creation. But something is missing: then God places man in the most beautiful garden that he might cultivate and look after it (cf. 2:15).

The Holy Spirit, who inspired the whole of the Bible, momentarily evokes the image of man alone - something is missing - without woman. And the Holy Spirit evokes God's thoughts, even his emotion, as he gazes at Adam, observing him alone in the garden. He is free, he is a lord... but he is alone. And God sees that this "is not good": as if what is missing is communion, he lacks communion, the fullness is lacking. "It is not good", God says, and adds: "I will make him a helper fit for him" (2:18).

Flesh of my flesh

And so God brings all the animals to man; man gives to each its name - and this is another image of man's dominion over creation - but he sees that not one of the animals is like himself. Man continues alone. When finally God presents woman, man exultantly recognises that this creature, and this creature alone, is a part of him: "bone of my bones and flesh of my flesh" (2:23). Finally, there is a reflection, a reciprocity. When a person - to give an example to help us understand - wants to shake hands with another, he must have that person before him: if he holds out his hand and no one is there…his hand remains outstretched, there is no reciprocity. This was how man was, he lacked something to reach his fullness; reciprocity was lacking. Woman is not a replica of man; she comes directly from the creative act of God. The image of the "rib" in no way expresses inferiority or subordination, but, on the contrary, that man and woman are of the same substance and are complementary and that they also have this reciprocity. And the fact that - also in that parable - God moulds woman while man sleeps means precisely that she is in no way man's creation, but God's. He also suggests another point: in order to find woman - and we could say to find love in woman - man first must dream of her and then find her. God's faith in man and in woman, those to whom he entrusted the earth, is generous, direct and full. He trusts them. But then the devil introduces suspicion into their minds, disbelief, distrust and finally, disobedience to the commandment that protected them. They fall into that delirium of omnipotence that pollutes everything and destroys harmony. We too feel it inside of us, all of us, frequently.

Negative excesses of patriarchal cultures

Sin generates distrust and division between man and woman. Their relationship will be undermined by a thousand forms of abuse and subjugation, misleading seduction and humiliating ignorance, even the most dramatic and violent kind. And history bears the scar. Let us think, for example, of those negative excesses of patriarchal cultures. Think of the many forms of male dominance whereby the woman was considered second class. Think of the exploitation and the commercialisation of the female body in the current media culture. And let us also think of the recent epidemic of distrust, scepticism and even hostility that is spreading in our culture - in particular an understandable distrust from women - on the part of a covenant between man and woman that is capable, at the same time, of refining the intimacy of communion and of guarding the dignity of difference.

If we do not find a surge of respect for this covenant, capable of protecting new generations from distrust and indifference, from children coming into the world ever more uprooted from the mother's womb. The social devaluation for the stable and generative alliance between man and woman is certainly a loss for everyone. We must return marriage and the family to the place of honour! The Bible says something beautiful: man finds woman, they meet and man must leave something in order to find her fully. That is why man will leave his father and mother to go to her. It's beautiful! This means setting out on a new path. Man is everything for woman and woman is everything for man.

The responsibility of guarding this covenant between man and woman is ours, although we are sinners and are wounded, confused and humiliated, discouraged and uncertain; it is nevertheless for us believers a demanding and gripping vocation in today's situation. The same narrative of creation and of sin ends by showing us an extremely beautiful icon: "The Lord God made for Adam and for his wife garments of skins, and clothed them" (*Gn* 3:21). It is an image of tenderness towards the sinful couple that leaves our mouths agape: the tenderness God has for man and woman! It's an image of fatherly care for the human couple. God himself cares for and protects his masterpiece.

MARRIAGE

Our reflection on *God's original plan for man and woman as a couple*, after having considered the two narratives from the Book of Genesis, now turns directly to Jesus.

At the beginning of his Gospel, John the Evangelist narrates the episode of the wedding at Cana, at which the Virgin Mary and Jesus were present with his first disciples (cf. *Jn* 2:1-11). Jesus not only participated at that wedding, but "saved the feast" with the miracle of wine! Thus, the first of his prodigious signs, with which he reveals his glory, he performed in the context of a wedding, and it was an act of great sympathy for that nascent family, entreated by Mary's motherly care. This reminds us of the Book of Genesis, when God completes his work of creation and makes his masterpiece; the masterpiece is man and woman. And here at a marriage, at a wedding feast, Jesus begins his own miracles with this masterpiece: a man and a woman. Thus Jesus teaches us that the masterpiece of society is the family: a man and a woman who love each other! This is the masterpiece!

Since the time of the wedding at Cana, many things have changed, but that "sign" of Christ contains an ever valid message. Today it seems difficult to speak of marriage as a feast which is renewed in time, in the various seasons of the couple's lifetime. It is a fact that progressively fewer people are getting married; this is a fact: young people don't want to get married. In many countries the number of separations is instead increasing while the number of children decreases. The difficulty of staying together - both as a couple and as a family - leads to bonds being broken with ever-increasing frequency and swiftness, and the children themselves are the first to suffer the consequences. Let us consider that the first victims, the most important victims, the victims who suffer the most in a separation are the children.

Culture of the provisional

Should you feel from childhood that marriage is a "temporary" bond, unconsciously it will be so for you. In fact, many young people are led to reject the very plan of an irrevocable bond and of a lasting family. I believe that we must reflect very seriously on why so many young people "don't feel like" getting married. There is a culture of the provisional...everything is provisional, it seems there is nothing definitive.

This matter of young people not wanting to marry is one of the emerging concerns of today: why aren't young people getting married? Why is it that they frequently prefer cohabitation and "limited responsibility"? Why is that many - even among the baptised - have little trust in marriage and in the family? If we want young people to be able to find the right road to follow, it is important to try to understand this. Why do they have no trust in the family?

The difficulties are not only economic, although these are truly serious. Many believe that the changes that have occurred in these last decades were put in motion by the emancipation of women. But even this argument is invalid, it's false, it isn't true! It is a form of male chauvinism, which always seeks to dominate women. We give the bad impression that Adam gave, when God asked him: "Why did you eat the fruit of the tree?" and he said: "The woman gave it to me". It's the woman's fault. The poor woman! We must defend women! In fact, nearly all men and women would want stable emotional security, a solid marriage and a happy family. The family tops all the indices of wellbeing among young people; but, fearing mistakes, many do not want to even consider it; even being Christians, they do not consider the Sacrament of Matrimony, the single and unrepeatable sign of the covenant, which becomes a testimony of faith. Perhaps this very fear of failure is the greatest obstacle to receiving the Word of Christ, which promises his grace to the conjugal union and to the family.

Christian seed at the root of equality

The most persuasive testimony of the blessing of Christian marriage is the good life of Christian spouses and of the family. There is no better way to speak of the beauty of the Sacrament! A marriage consecrated by God safeguards that bond between man and woman that God has blessed from the very creation of the world; and it is the source of peace and goodness for the entire lifetime of the marriage and family. For example, in the first ages of Christianity, this great dignity of the bond between man and woman overcame an abuse then held normal, namely the husbands' right to repudiate their wives, even for reasons based on pretext or to humiliate. The Gospel of the family, the Gospel which proclaims this very Sacrament overcame this culture of customary repudiation.

The Christian seed at the root of equality between spouses must bear new fruit today. The witness of the social dignity of marriage shall become persuasive precisely in this way, the way of a testimony which attracts, the way of reciprocity between them, of complementarity between them.

For this reason, as Christians, we must become more demanding in this regard. For example: firmly support the right to equal pay for equal work; why is it taken for granted that women should earn less than men? No! They have the same rights. This disparity is an absolute disgrace! At the same time, recognise women's motherhood and men's fatherhood as an always precious treasure, for the good of their children above all. Likewise, the virtue of the hospitality of Christian families today takes on a crucial importance, especially in situations of poverty, degradation and domestic violence.

Dear brothers and sisters, do not be afraid to invite Jesus to your wedding feast, to invite Him to our home, that He may be with us and safeguard the family. And we mustn't be afraid to also invite his Mother Mary! When Christians marry "in the Lord", they are transformed into an effective sign of God's love. Christians do not marry for themselves alone: they marry in the Lord for the good of the entire community, society as a whole.

THE BEAUTY OF CHRISTIAN MARRIAGE

In our journey of catecheses on the family, today we touch directly *on the beauty of Christian marriage*. It is not merely a ceremony in a church, with flowers, a dress, photographs…. Christian marriage is a sacrament that takes place *in* the Church, and which also *makes* the Church, by giving rise to a new family community.

It is what the Apostle Paul says in his celebrated expression: "This mystery is a profound one, and I am saying that it refers to Christ and the Church" (*Ep* 5:32). Inspired by the Holy Spirit, Paul says that the love between spouses is an image of the love between Christ and his Church. An unimaginable dignity! But in fact it is inscribed in the creative design of God, and with the grace of Christ innumerable Christian couples, with all their limitations and sins, have realised it!

St Paul, speaking of new life in Christ, says that Christians - each one of them - are called to love one another as Christ has loved them, that is to "be subject to one another" (*Ep* 5:21), which means be at the service of one another. And here he introduces an analogy between husband-wife and Christ-Church. It is clear that this is an imperfect analogy, but we must take it in the spiritual sense which is very lofty and revolutionary, and at the same time simple, available to every man and woman who entrusts him and herself to the grace of God.

Husbands - Paul says - must love their wives "as their own body" (*Ep* 5:28); to love them as Christ "loved the Church and gave himself up for her" (v. 25). You husbands who are present here, do you understand this? Do you love your wives as Christ loves the Church? This is no joke, these are serious things! The effect of this radical devotion asked of man, for the love and dignity of woman, following the example of Christ, must have been tremendous in the Christian community itself. This seed of evangelical novelty, which re-establishes the original reciprocity of devotion and respect, matured throughout history slowly but ultimately it prevailed.

To love unconditionally

The Sacrament of Marriage is a great act of faith and love: a witness to the courage to believe in the beauty of the creative act of God and to live that love that is always urging us to go on, beyond ourselves and even beyond our own family. The Christian vocation to love unconditionally and without limit is what, by the grace of Christ, is also at the foundation of the free consent that constitutes marriage.

The Church herself is fully involved in the story of every Christian marriage: she is built on their successes and she suffers in their failures. But we must ask in all seriousness: do we ourselves as believers and as pastors, accept deep down this indissoluble bond of the history of Christ and his Church with the history of marriage and the human family? Are we seriously ready to take up this responsibility, that is, that every marriage goes on the path of the love that Christ has for the Church? This is a great thing!

In the depths of this mystery of creation, acknowledged and restored in its purity, opens a second great horizon that marks the Sacrament of Marriage. The decision to "wed in the Lord" also entails a missionary dimension, which means having at heart the willingness to be a medium for God's blessing and for the Lord's grace *to all*. Indeed, Christian spouses participate *as spouses* in the mission of the Church. This takes courage! That is why when I meet newlyweds, I say: "Here are the brave ones!" because it takes courage to love one another as Christ loves the Church.

Church's great mission of love

The celebration of the Sacrament must have this co-responsibility of family life in the Church's great mission of love. And thus the life of the Church is enriched every time by the beauty of this spousal covenant, and deteriorates every time it is disfigured. The Church, in order to offer to all the gifts of faith, hope and love, needs the courageous fidelity of spouses to the grace of their sacrament! The People of God need their daily journey in faith, in love and in hope, with all the joys and the toils that this journey entails in a marriage and a family.

The route is well marked forever, it is the route of love: to love as God loves, forever. Christ does not cease to care for the Church: he loves her always, he guards her always, as himself. Christ does not cease to remove stains and lines of every kind from the human face. Moving and very beautiful to see is this radiation of God's power and tenderness which is transmitted from couple to couple, family to family. St Paul is right: this truly is a "great mystery"! Men and women, brave enough to carry this treasure in the "earthen vessels" of our humanity, are - these men and these women who are so brave - an essential resource for the Church, as well as for the world! May God bless them a thousand times over for this!

THE THREE EXPRESSIONS

Today's catechesis will serve as a doorway to a series of reflections on family life and what it's really like to live in a family, day in and day out. Imagine three expressions written above the doorway; expressions I've already mentioned here in St Peter's Square several times before. The expressions are: "may I?", "thank you" and "pardon me". Indeed, these expressions open up the way to living well in your family, to living in peace. They are simple expressions, but so simple to put into practice! They hold much power: the power to keep home life intact even when tested with a thousand problems. But if they are absent, little holes can start to crack open and the whole thing may even collapse.

We usually include these expressions under the general category of being "well-mannered". Okay, a well-mannered person asks permission, says thanks and asks forgiveness after making a mistake. Very well. But good manners really are that important. A great Bishop, St Francis de Sales, used to say that "good manners are are already half the way to holiness". But be careful: history has shown that good manners also can become a kind of formalism that masks a dryness of soul and indifference towards the other person. It is often said: "behind a lot of good manners lurk a lot of bad habits." Not even religion is immune from the risk of having formal observance sink into spiritual worldliness. The devil, tempting Jesus, boasts of good manners. Indeed, he presents himself as a gentleman, a knight in shining armour. He even presents himself as a theologian by quoting Holy Scripture. He appears to have everything right and neat on the outside, but his intent is always to lead others astray from the truth of God's love. We, however, mean "good manners" only in the most authentic way, according to which the habit of cultivating good relations is firmly rooted in a love for the good and a respect for the other person. The family lives according to this refined sense of loving.

May I?

Let's look at these expressions: the first expression is "may I?" When we take care to ask for something kindly - even something we think we have a rightful claim to - we help to strengthen the common life that undergirds marriage and the family. Entering into the life of another, even when that person already has a part to play in our life, demands the sensitivity of a non-invasive attitude which renews trust and respect. Indeed, the deeper and more intimate love is, the more it calls for respect for the other's freedom and the ability to wait until the other opens the door to his or her heart. At this point, we can remember the words of Jesus in the Book of Revelation: "Behold, I stand at the door and knock; if any one hears my voice and opens the door, I will come in to him and eat with him, and he with me" (3:20). Even the Lord asks permission to enter! Let us not forget that. Before doing anything in your family, ask: "Do you mind if I do this? Would you like me to do this?" This way of asking is well-mannered indeed, but it is also full of love. This does so much good for families.

Thank you

The second expression is "thank you". Sometimes we have to wonder if we are turning into a civilisation of bad manners and bad words, as if this were a sign of self-liberation. It's not uncommon to hear these bad words publicly. Kindness and the ability to say "thank you" are often considered a sign of weakness and raise the suspicion of others. This tendency is encountered even within the nucleus of the family. We must become firmly determined to educate others to be grateful and appreciative: the dignity of the person and social justice must both pass through the portal of the family. If family life neglects this style of living, social life will also reject it. Gratitude, however, stands at the very core of the faith of the believer. A Christian who does not know how to thank has lost the very "language" of God. This is terrible! Let's not forget Jesus' question after he heals the ten lepers and only one of them returns to thank him (Lk 17:18). I remember once listening to a very wise, old person; very simple, but with that uncommon wisdom of life and piety: "Gratitude is a plant that grows only in the soil of noble souls." That nobility of soul, that grace of God in the soul compels us to say "thank you" with gratitude. It is the flower of a noble soul. This really is something beautiful.

I'm sorry

The third expression is "pardon me". Granted, it's not always easy to say, but it is so necessary. Whenever it is lacking, the little cracks begin to open up - even when we don't want them to - and they can even become enormous sinkholes. It's hardly insignificant that in the "Our Father" that Jesus teaches us - a prayer that sums up all of life's essential questions - we find this expression: "Forgive us our trespasses, as we forgive those who trespass against us" (*Mt* 6:12). To acknowledge that we have fallen short, to be desirous of returning that which has been taken away - respect, sincerity, love - these make us worthy of pardon. This is how we heal the infection. If we are not able to forgive ourselves, then we are no longer able to forgive full stop. A house in which the words "I'm sorry" are never uttered begins to lack air, and the flood waters begin to choke those who live inside. So many wounds, so many scrapes and bruises are the result of a lack of these precious words: "I am sorry". Marital life is so often torn apart by fights…the "plates will even start flying", but let me give you a word of advice: never finish the day without making peace with one another. Listen to me carefully: did you fight with your wife or husband? Kids - did you fight with your parents? Did you seriously argue? That's not a good thing, but it's not really that which is the problem: the problem arises only if this feeling hangs over into the next day. So if you've fought, do not let the day end without making peace with your family. And how am I going to make peace? By getting down on my knees? No! Just by a small gesture, a little something, and harmony within your family will be restored. Just a little caress, no words necessary. But don't let the sun go down on your family without having made your peace. Do you understand me? It's not easy, but you have to do it. It will help to make life so much more beautiful.

So these three key expressions for family life are really simple words; so simple that perhaps they even bring a smile to our face. But when we forget them, it's no laughing matter, right? Perhaps we overlook our good manners too often. May the Lord help us to put them back where they belong: in our hearts, in our homes and in our civic life. These are the words that truly enter into the love of a family.

EDUCATION

Today, dear brothers and sisters, I would like to welcome you because I saw among you many families. Good morning to all the families! Let us continue to reflect on the family. Today we will pause to reflect on an essential characteristic of the family, the natural vocation to *educate children* so they may grow up to be responsible for themselves and for others. What we heard from the Apostle Paul, at the start, is very beautiful: "Children, obey your parents in everything, for this pleases the Lord. Fathers, do not provoke your children, lest they become discouraged" (*Col* 3:20-21). This is a wise rule: children should be raised to listen to their parents and obey their parents, who, in turn, should not order them around in a negative way, so as not to discourage the children. Children, indeed, must grow without becoming discouraged, step by step. If you parents say to your children: "Let's climb this ladder" and you take them by the hand and, step by step, help them climb, things will go well. But if you say: "Go up!" - "But I can't" - "Go!" This is called provoking your children, asking them to do things they don't have the ability to do. That is why the relationship between parents and children must be one of wisdom, of a great balance. Children, obey your parents, this pleases God. And you parents, don't provoke your children by asking of them things they can't do. And this needs to be done so that children can grow up to be responsible for themselves and for others.

It would seem like an obvious statement, there are difficulties still in our times. It is hard to educate when parents only see their children in the evening, when they come home tired from work. Well, those who are fortunate enough to work! It is even more difficult for parents who are separated, who are weighed down by their condition: the poor dears, they have had real hardships, they have separated and frequently the child is taken hostage and the father speaks ill of the mother, and the mother speaks ill of the father, and so much harm is done. But I say to separated parents: never, never, never take your child hostage! You separated because of many difficulties and reasons, life has given you this trial, but the children should not be the ones to carry the weight of this separation, they should not be used as hostages against the other spouse, they should grow up hearing their mother speak well of their father, even though they are not together, and the father speak well of their mother. For separated parents this is very important and very difficult, but they can do it.

How should we educate?

Above all, the question is: how should we educate? What tradition do we have today to pass onto our children?

Intellectual "critics" of every kind have silenced parents in countless ways, in order to protect the younger generations from the damage - real or presumed - of family education. The family stands accused, among other things, of being authoritarian, of favouritism, of conformism, of the emotional repression that generates conflict.

In fact, a rift has opened up between the family and society, between the family and school, the educational pact today has been broken; and thus, the educational alliance between society and the family is in crisis because mutual trust has been undermined. There are many symptoms. For example, at school relationships between parents and teachers have been compromised. At times there is tension and mutual distrust; and naturally, the consequences fall on the children. On the other hand, the number of so-called "experts" has multiplied, and they have assumed the role of parents in even the most intimate aspects of education. With regard to emotional life, personality and development, rights and duties, these "experts" know everything: objectives, motivations, techniques. And parents must simply listen, learn and adapt. Deprived of their role, they often become overly apprehensive and possessive of their children, to the point of never correcting them: "You cannot correct the child." They tend to entrust them more and more to the "experts", even in the most delicate and personal aspects of their lives, putting themselves alone in a corner; and thus parents today run the risk of excluding themselves from the lives of their children. And this is very grave! Today there are cases like this. I am not saying that it always happens, but there are cases. The teacher will admonish the child at school and send a note to the parents. I remember a personal anecdote. Once, when I was in the fourth grade, I said a bad word to the teacher and the teacher, being a good woman, called my mum. She came the next day, they spoke together, and then I was called. And my mother explained to me in front of the teacher that what I had done was bad, that I shouldn't have done it; but my mother did it with such sweetness and she asked me to apologise to the teacher in front of her. I did it and then I was glad that I did: the story had a happy ending. But that was only the first chapter! When I got home, the second chapter began…. Imagine today if a teacher were to do something of the kind, the next day the parents, or one of the two, would seek to admonish her, because the "experts" say that children should not be reproached like this. Things have changed! That is why parents should not exclude themselves from their children's education.

Where are children on their journey?

It is clear that this approach is not good: it is not harmony, it is not dialogue, and rather than fostering co-operation between the family and other educational agencies, schools, gymnasiums… it counteracts it.

How did we get to this point? There is no doubt that parents or, better yet, certain past educational models had their limitations, there is no doubt. But it is also true that there are mistakes that only parents are allowed to make, because they can compensate for them in a way that is impossible for anyone else. On the other hand, as we well know, life has become stingy with the time for talking, reflecting and facing oneself. Many parents are "sequestered" by work - mum and dad have to work - and by worries, uncomfortable with the new needs of their children and with the complexity of modern life - which is the way it is and we must accept it as it is - and they find themselves as if paralysed by the fear of making a mistake. The problem, however, is not just talking. Superficial "dialogue" does not lead to a true meeting of mind and heart. Let us ask instead: do we seek to understand "where" our children really are in their journey? Where is their soul, do we really know? And above all: do we want to know? Are we convinced that they, in reality, aren't waiting for something else?

The foundation of everything is love

Christian communities are called to offer support to the educational mission of families, and they do this first of all with the light of the Word of God. The Apostle Paul recalls the reciprocity of duties between parents and children: "Children, obey your parents in everything, for this pleases the Lord. Fathers, do not provoke your children, lest they become discouraged" (*Col* 3:20-21). At the foundation of everything is love, that which God gives us, which "is not arrogant or rude. Love does not insist on its own way; it is not irritable or resentful; it does not rejoice at wrong, but... bears all things, believes all things, hopes all things, endures all things" (1 *Co* 13:5-7). Even the best families need support, and it takes a lot of patience to support one another! But such is life. Life is not lived in a laboratory, but in reality. Jesus himself experienced a family upbringing.

Also in this case, the grace of the love of Christ leads to the fulfilment of what is inscribed in human nature. How many astounding examples we have of Christian parents filled with human wisdom! They show that a good family upbringing is the backbone of humanity. Its radiance in society is the source that allows us to fill in the gaps, wounds and voids in parenthood that affect less fortunate children. This radiance can work real miracles. And in the Church these miracles happen every day!

I hope that the Lord bestows on Christian families the faith, freedom and courage necessary for their mission. If family education rediscovers the pride of its leadership, many things will change for the better, for uncertain parents and for disappointed children. It is time for fathers and mothers to return from their exile - for they have exiled themselves from their children's upbringing - and to fully resume their educational role. We hope that the Lord gives this grace to parents: to not exile themselves from the education of their children. And this can only be done with love, tenderness and patience.

ENGAGEMENT

Continuing these catecheses on the family, today I would like to speak about *engagement*. Engagement - one hears it in the word - has to do with trust, confidence, reliability. Confidence in the vocation that God gives, since marriage is first and foremost the discovery of a call from God. Certainly it is a beautiful thing that young people today can choose to marry on the basis of mutual love. But the very freedom of the bond requires a conscious harmony in the decision, not just a simple understanding of the attraction or feeling, for a moment, for a short time...it calls for a journey.

Engagement, in other words, is the time when the two are called to perform a real labour of love, an involved and shared work that delves deep. Here they discover one another little by little, i.e. the man "learns" about woman by learning about *this* woman, his fiancée; and the woman "learns" about man by learning about *this* man, her fiancé. Let us not underestimate the importance of this learning: it is a beautiful endeavour, and love itself requires it, for it is not simply a matter of carefree happiness or enchanted emotion. The biblical account speaks of all creation as a beautiful work of God's love. The Book of Genesis says that: "God saw everything that he had made, and behold, it was very good" (*Gn* 1:31). Only when it is finished does God "rest". We understand from this image that God's love, which brought forth the world, was not an impromptu decision. No! It was a beautiful work. The love of God created the concrete conditions for an irrevocable covenant, one that is strong and lasting.

Covenant for life

The covenant of love between man and woman - a covenant for life - *cannot be improvised*. It isn't made up one day to the next. There is no marriage express: one needs to work on love, one needs to walk. The covenant of love between man and woman is something learned and refined. I venture to say it is a covenant carefully crafted. To make two lives one is almost a miracle of freedom and the heart entrusted to faith. Perhaps we should emphasise this point more, because our "emotional co-ordinates" have gone a bit askew. Those who claim to want everything right away, then back out of everything - right away - at the first difficulty (or at the first opportunity). There is no hope for the trust and fidelity entailed in the gift of self, if the prevailing tendency is to consume love like some kind of "supplement" for mental and physical well being. This is not love! Engagement focuses on the will to care for something together that must never be bought or sold, betrayed or abandoned, however tempting the offer may be.

God, too, when he speaks of the covenant with his people, does so several times in terms of betrothal. In the Book of Jeremiah, in speaking to the people who had distanced themselves from him, he reminds the people of when they were the "betrothed" of God, and he says: "I remember the devotion of your youth, your love as a bride" (cf. 2:2). God took this path of betrothal. He then also made a promise: we heard it at the beginning of the audience, in the Book of Hosea: "I will betroth you to me forever; I will betroth you to me in righteousness and in justice, in steadfast love, and in mercy. I will betroth you to me in faithfulness; and you shall know the Lord" (2:19-20).

What a long road!

The road the Lord takes with his people on this betrothal journey is a long one. At the end, God espouses his people in Jesus Christ. In Jesus he marries the Church. The People of God is Jesus' Bride. But what a long road! And you Italians, in your literature you have a masterpiece on betrothal, *The Betrothed*. Young people need to know about it and read it. It is a masterpiece that tells the story of an engaged couple who have endured great suffering, they travel a road filled with many struggles, until at last they arrive at marriage. Don't leave aside this masterpiece on betrothal, which Italian literature has given especially to you. Go on, read it and you will see the beauty, the suffering, but also the faithfulness of the betrothed.

The Church, in her wisdom, guards the *distinction between being engaged and being spouses* - it's not the same - especially in view of the delicateness and depth of this test. Let us be careful not to disregard light-heartedly the wisdom of this teaching, which also comes from the experience of happy married life. The powerful symbols of the body hold the keys to the soul: we cannot treat the bonds of the flesh lightly, without opening some lasting wound in the spirit (cf. 1 *Co* 6:15-20).

Of course, today's culture and society have become rather indifferent to the delicateness and seriousness of this step. On the other hand, it cannot be said that they are generous to young people who are determined to make a home and welcome children. Indeed, often they put up a thousand obstacles, both psychological and practical. Engagement is a path of life that has to ripen like fruit; it is a way of maturing in love, until the moment it becomes marriage.

Sharing a plan

Pre-marriage courses are a special expression of preparation. And we see so many couples, who perhaps come to the course somewhat reluctantly: "But these priests make us take a course! But why? We already know..." and they go reluctantly. But afterwards they are happy and grateful, because they have found there the opportunity - sometimes the only one - to reflect on their experience in non-trivial terms. Yes, many couples are together a long time, perhaps also in intimacy, sometimes living together, but *they don't really know each other*. It seems curious, but experience shows that it's true. Therefore engagement needs to be re-evaluated as a time of getting to know one another and sharing a plan. The path of preparation for marriage should be implemented from this perspective, also with the benefit of the simple but intense witness of Christian spouses. And also by focusing on the essentials: the Bible, by consciously rediscovering it together; prayer, in its liturgical dimension, but also in "domestic prayer" to live out in the home, the Sacraments, the sacramental life, Confession…where the Lord comes to abide in the engaged couple and prepare them truly to receive one another "with the grace of Christ"; and fraternity with the poor and those in need, who lead us to live soberly and to share.

Step by step

Engaged couples who commit themselves to this path both grow, and all of this leads to preparing for a beautiful celebration of marriage in a different way, not in a worldly way, but in a Christian way! Let us consider these words of God we have heard, when he speaks to his people as bridegroom to his future bride: "I will betroth you to me forever; I will betroth you to me in righteousness and in justice, in steadfast love, and in mercy. I will betroth you to me in faithfulness; and you shall know the Lord" (*Ho* 2:19-20). May every engaged couple think of this and say to one another: "I will take you as my bride, I will take you as my bridegroom." Wait for that moment. It is a moment, it is a path that goes slowly ahead, but it is a path of maturation. The steps of the journey should not be rushed. This is how we mature, step by step.

The time of betrothal can truly become a time of initiation, into what? Into surprise. Into the surprise of the spiritual gifts with which the Lord, through the Church, enriches the horizon of the new family that stands ready to live in his blessing.

I invite you now to pray to the Holy Family of Nazareth: Jesus, Joseph and Mary. Pray that the family may make this journey of preparation; and pray for couples who are betrothed. Let us pray to Our Lady all together, a Hail Mary for all engaged couples, that they may understand the beauty of this journey towards marriage.

FAMILY AND POVERTY

In these catecheses we have been reflecting on the family and we continue forward with this topic, reflecting on the family. As of today, our catecheses open onto the consideration of the vulnerability of the family, in the living conditions that put it to the test. So many problems are testing families.

One of these trials is poverty. Let us think of the many families that live on the outskirts of major cities, as well as those in rural areas.... So much misery, so much degradation! And then, to make the situation worse, in some places there is also war. War is always a terrible thing. Moreover, it also strikes above all the civil populations, the families. Truly, war is the "mother of all poverty", war impoverishes the family, a great predator of lives, souls and of the most sacred and beloved bonds.

Despite all this, there are many poor families who try to live their daily lives with dignity, often openly entrusting themselves to God's blessing. This lesson, however, should not justify our indifference, but rather increase our shame over the fact that there is so much poverty! It is almost a miracle that, even in poverty, the family continues to form, and even preserve - as much as it can - the special humanity of those bonds. This fact irritates those planners of wellbeing who consider attachments, procreation and familial bonds as secondary variables to the quality of life. They don't understand a thing! On the contrary, we should kneel down before these families, who are a true school of humanity in saving societies from barbarity.

Boundless work of the family

What do we have left if we yield to the extortion of Caesar and Mammon, to violence and to money, and renounce even family ties? A new civil ethic will arrive only when the leaders of public life reorganise the social bond beginning with the perverse struggle that spirals between the family and poverty, which leads us into the abyss.

The prevailing economy is often concentrated on the enjoyment of individual wellbeing, but it largely exploits family ties. This is a serious contradiction! The boundless work of the family is not quoted in financial statements, obviously! Indeed economics and politics are misers with regard to acknowledging this. Yet, the interior formation of the person and the social flow of affections have their mainstay precisely there. Should it be removed, everything would fall apart.

It is not merely a question of bread. We are talking about work, talking about education, talking about health. It is important that this be clearly understood. We are always quite moved when we see images of sick and malnourished children that are shown in so many parts of the world. At the same time, we are also deeply moved by the twinkle in the eyes of many children, deprived of everything and in schools built from nothing, who are proud when showing off their pencil and their notebook. And how lovingly they look at their teacher! Children already know that man does not live on bread alone! And as for family affection; when there is destitution children suffer because they want love, family ties.

Social destitution strikes the family

We Christians have to be ever closer to the families whom poverty puts to the test. But think, all of you know someone: a father without work, a mother without work…and this makes the family suffer, the bonds are weakened. This is terrible. Indeed, *social destitution strikes the family and sometimes destroys it*. The lack, loss or strong instability of employment weigh heavily upon family life, imposing a substantial strain on relationships. Living conditions in the poorest neighbourhoods, with housing and transportation problems, as well as reduced social, health and educational services, bring about further difficulties. Adding to these material factors is the damage caused to the family by the pseudo-models spread by the mass media on the basis of consumerism and the cult of appearances, which influence the poorest social classes and increase the breakdown of family ties. Take care of families, attend to the attachment, when destitution puts the family to the test!

Prayer and action are needed

The Church is Mother, and must not forget this drama of her children. She too must be poor, to become fruitful and respond to so much poverty. A poor Church is a Church that practises voluntary simplicity in her life - in her very institutions, in the lifestyle of her members - to break down every dividing wall, especially to the poor. Prayer and action are needed. Let us pray earnestly that the Lord stir us, to render our Christian families leaders of this revolution of familial proximity, that is now so essential for us! The Church is made of it, of this familial proximity. Let us not forget that the judgement of the needy, of the small and of the poor prefigures the judgement of God (*Mt* 25:31-46). Let's not forget this and let's do all we can to help families to go forward in the trial of poverty and destitution which strikes attachments and family bonds. I would like to read once again the Bible test that we heard at the beginning, and each of us think about the families who are tried by destitution and poverty, the Bible reads like this: "My son, deprive not the poor of his living, and do not keep needy eyes waiting. Do not grieve the one who is hungry, nor anger a man in want. Do not add to the troubles of an angry mind, nor delay your gift to a beggar. Do not reject an afflicted suppliant, nor turn your face away from the poor. Do not avert your eye from the needy, nor give a man occasion to curse you" (*Si* 4:1-5a). For this is what the Lord will do - so it says in the Gospel - if we do not do these things.

FAMILY AND ILLNESS

We continue the catecheses on the family, and in this catechesis I would like to touch upon a condition common to all families, namely, illness. It is an experience of our own fragility, which we experience most of all at home, beginning in childhood, and then especially in the aches and pains of old age. Within the realm of family bonds, the illness of our loved ones is endured with an "excess" of suffering and anguish. It is love that makes us feel this "excess". So often for a father or a mother, it is more difficult to bear a son or daughter's pain than one's own. The family, we can say, has always been the nearest "hospital". Still today, in so many parts of the world, a hospital is for the privileged few, and is often far away. It is the mother, the father, brothers, sisters and grandparents who guarantee care and help one to heal.

In the Gospels, many pages tell of Jesus' encounters with the sick and of his commitment to healing them. He presents himself publicly as one who fights against illness and who has come to heal mankind of every evil: evils of the spirit and evils of the body. The Gospel scene just referenced from the Gospel according to Mark is truly moving. It says: "That evening, at sundown, they brought

to him all who were sick or possessed with demons"
(1:32). When I think of today's great cities, I wonder where
are the doors to which the sick are brought hoping to be
healed! Jesus never held back from their care. He never
passed by, never turned his face away. When a father or
mother, or even just friends brought a sick person for him
to touch and heal, he never let time be an issue; healing
came before the law, even one as sacred as resting on the
Sabbath (cf. *Mk* 3:1-6). The doctors of the law reproached
Jesus because he healed on the Sabbath, he did good on the
Sabbath. But the love of Jesus was in giving health, doing
good: this always takes priority!

This is the task

Jesus sends his disciples to perform the same work and
gives them the power to heal, in other words, to draw close
to the sick and to heal their deepest wounds (cf. *Mt* 10:1).
We must keep in mind what he says to the disciples in
the episode of the man blind from birth (*Jn* 9:1-5). The
disciples - with the blind man there in front of them! - argue
about who sinned, this man or his parents, that he was born
blind, causing his blindness. The Lord says clearly: neither
him nor his parents; he is so in order that the works of God
be made manifest in him. And he heals him. This is the
glory of God! This is the Church's task! To help the sick,
not to get lost in gossip, always help, comfort, relieve, be
close to the sick; this is the task.

The Church invites constant prayer for her own loved ones stricken with suffering. There must never be a lack of prayer for the sick. But rather, we must pray more, both personally and as a community. Let us consider the Gospel episode of the Canaanite woman (cf. *Mt* 15:21-28). She is a pagan woman. She is not of the People of Israel, but a pagan who implores Jesus to heal her daughter. To test her faith, Jesus at first responds harshly: "I cannot, I must think first of the sheep of Israel". The woman does not give up - when a mother asks for help for her infant, she never gives up; we all know that mothers fight for their children - and she replies: "even dogs are given something when their masters have eaten", as if to say: "At least treat me like a dog!" Thus Jesus says to her: "woman, great is your faith! Be it done for you as you desire" (v. 28).

Solidarity

In the face of illness, even in families, difficulties arise due to human weakness. But in general, times of illness enable family bonds to grow stronger. I think about how important it is to teach children, starting from childhood, about solidarity in times of illness. An education which protects against sensitivity for human illness withers the heart. It allows young people to be "anaesthetised" against the suffering of others, incapable of facing suffering and of living the experience of limitation. How often do we see a man or woman arrive at work with a weary face, with a tired countenance and, when we ask them: "What happened?" they answer: "I only slept two hours because we are taking turns at home to be close to our boy, our girl, our sick one, our grandfather, our grandmother." And the day of work goes on. These are heroic deeds, the heroism of families! That hidden heroism carried out with tenderness and courage when someone at home is sick.

The weakness and suffering of our dearest and most cherished loved ones can be, for our children and grandchildren, a school of life - it's important to teach the children, the grandchildren to understand this closeness in illness at home - and they become so when times of illness are accompanied by prayer and the affectionate and thoughtful closeness of relatives. The Christian community really knows that the family, in the trial of illness, should not be left on its own. We must say "thank you" to the Lord for those beautiful experiences of ecclesial fraternity that help families get through the difficult moments of pain and suffering. This Christian closeness, from family to family, is a real treasure for the parish; a treasure of wisdom, which helps families in the difficult moments to understand the Kingdom of God better than many discourses! They are God's caresses.

DEATH

In the course of our catecheses on the family, today we take direct inspiration from the episode narrated by Luke the Evangelist, which we have just heard (cf. *Lk* 7:11-15). It is a very moving scene, which shows us Christ's compassion for those who suffer - in this case a widow who has lost her only child - and it also shows us Jesus' power over death.

Death is an experience which touches all families, without exception. It is part of life; yet, where familial love is concerned, death never seems natural. For parents, surviving their own children is particularly heart-breaking; it contradicts the fundamental nature of the very relationships that give meaning to the family. The loss of a son or daughter is like time stopping altogether: it opens a chasm that swallows both past and future. Death, which takes away a little child or young person, is a blow to the promises, to the gifts and the sacrifices of love joyfully brought to the life we gave birth to. Frequently parents come to Mass at Santa Marta with the photo of a son, a daughter, a baby, a boy, a girl, and they say to me: "He's gone, she's gone." And their faces are filled with grief. Death touches us and when it is a child's, it touches us profoundly. The whole family is left paralysed, speechless.

And the child left alone by the loss of one or both parents suffers in a similar way. She asks: "Where is my daddy? Where is my mama?" - "Well, she is in heaven" - "Why can't I see her?" This question covers the agony in the heart of a child left alone. The emptiness of abandonment that opens up in him is made all the more agonising by the fact that he doesn't have the life experience to even "give a name" to what has happened. "When is daddy coming back?" When is mama coming?" What do you say when a child suffers? This is what death in the family is like.

Death is like a hole

In these cases, death is like a black hole that opens up in the life of the family and for which we have no explanation. And at times we even go so far as to lay the blame on God. How many people - I understand them - get angry with God, blaspheme: "Why did you take my son, my daughter? There is no God, God does not exist! Why did he do this?" We hear this so often. But this anger is basically what comes from the heart in great pain; the loss of a son or of a daughter, of a father or of a mother, is a great sorrow. This happens over and over in families. In these cases, I said, death is like a hole. But physical death has "accomplices" even worse than itself, which are called hate, envy, pride, greed; in short, the sin of the world which works for death and makes it even more painful and unjust. Family bonds seem to be the predestined and helpless victims of these helping powers of death, trailing the history of mankind. Let us think of the absurd "normality" with which, at certain moments and in certain places, events adding to the horror of death are provoked by the hatred and indifference of other human beings. May the Lord keep us free from being accustomed to this!

Death does not have the last word

In the People of God, by the grace of his compassion granted in Jesus, many families prove by their deeds that death does not have the last word: this is a true act of faith. Every time a family in mourning - even terrible mourning - finds the strength to guard the faith and love that unite us to those we love, it has already prevented death from taking everything. The darkness of death should be confronted with a more intense work of love. "My God, lighten my darkness!" is the invocation of evening prayer. In the light of the Resurrection of the Lord, who abandons none of those whom the Father entrusted to him, we can take the "sting" out of death, as the Apostle Paul says (1 *Co* 15:55); we can prevent it from poisoning life, from rendering vain our love, from pushing us into the darkest chasm.

In this faith, we can console one another, knowing that the Lord has conquered death once and for all. Our loved ones are not lost in the darkness of nothing: hope assures us that they are in the good and strong hands of God. Love is stronger than death. Thus, the way is to let love grow, make it stronger, and love will guard us until the day that every tear shall be wiped away, when "death shall be no more, neither shall there be mourning nor crying nor pain any more" (*Rv* 21:4). If we allow ourselves to be sustained by this faith, the experience of grief can generate even stronger family bonds, a new openness to the pain of other families, a new brotherhood with families that are born and reborn in hope. To be born and reborn in hope, this gives us faith. But I would like to stress the last phrase of the Gospel which he heard today (cf. *Lk* 7:11-15). After Jesus brought the young man, the only son of a widow, back to life, the Gospel says: "Jesus gave him back to his mother". And this is our hope! All our loved ones who are gone, the Lord will give them back to us and we will be together with them. This hope does not disappoint! Let us remember well this action of Jesus: "And Jesus gave him back to his mother", thus the Lord will do with all our loved ones in the family!

We must weep in mourning

This faith protects us from the nihilist vision of death, as well as from the false consolations of the world, so that the Christian truth "does not risk mixing itself with myths of various types", surrendering to superstitions beliefs (Benedict XVI, *Angelus*, 2nd November 2008). Today it is necessary that pastors and all Christians express in a more concrete way the meaning of the faith with regard to the family experience of grief. We should not deny them the right to weep - we must weep in mourning - "Jesus wept" and was "deeply troubled" by the grave loss of a family that he loved (cf. *Jn* 11:33-37). We can draw from the simple and strong testimony of the many families who have been able to grasp, in the most arduous transition of death, the safe passage of the Lord, Crucified and Risen, with his irrevocable promise of the resurrection of the dead. God's work of love is stronger than the work of death. It is of that love, it is precisely of that love, that we must make ourselves hardworking "accomplices", with our faith! And let us remember Jesus' deed: "And Jesus gave him back to his mother", so he will do with all our loved ones and with us when we meet again, when death will be definitively conquered in us. It was conquered by Jesus' Cross. Jesus will give us all back to the family!

Wounds

In recent catecheses we have spoken about the family suffering through the frailties of the human condition, poverty, sickness and death. Today, however, we will reflect on the hurts that are incurred in family life. When, that is, we hurt one another within the family. The worst thing!

We know that in every family history there are moments in which the intimacy of loved ones is offended by the behaviour of its members. Words and actions (and omissions!) that, rather than expressing love, dismiss it or even mortify it. When these hurts, which are still rectifiable, are ignored, they deepen: they transform into impertinence, hostility and contempt. And at that point they can become deep wounds that divide husband and wife, and induce them to find understanding, support, consolation elsewhere. But often these "supports" do not consider the good of the family!

The depletion of conjugal love spreads resentment in relationships. And often this disintegration "collapses" onto the children.

There: the children. I would like to meditate a little on this point. Despite our seemingly evolved sensitivity, and all our refined psychological analyses, I ask myself if we are not just anaesthetising ourselves to the wounds in children's souls. The more you try to compensate with gifts and snacks, the more you lose your sense of these spiritual wounds - so painful and so deep. We talk a lot about behavioural problems, mental health, the wellbeing of the child, about the anxiety of parents and their children.... But do we even know what a spiritual wound is? Do we feel the weight of the mountain that crushes the soul of a child in those families where members mistreat and hurt one another to the point of breaking the bonds of marital fidelity. How much weight, do our choices have - mistaken choices, for example - how much weight do they place on the soul of our children? When adults lose their heads, when each one thinks only of him - or herself, when a dad and mum hurt one another, the souls of their children suffer terribly, they experience a sense of despair. And these wounds leave a mark that lasts their whole lives.

Everything is connected

In the family, everything is connected: when her soul is wounded in some way, the infection spreads to everyone. And when a man and a woman, who have committed to being "one flesh" and forming a family, think obsessively of their own need for freedom and gratification, this bias affects the hearts and lives of their children in a profound way. Frequently these children hide to cry alone.... We need to understand this fully. Husband and wife are one flesh. Their own little children are flesh of their flesh. If we think of the harshness with which Jesus admonishes adults not to scandalise the little ones - we heard the Gospel passage (cf. *Mt* 18:6) - we can also better understand his words on the serious responsibility to guard the marital bond that gives rise to the human family (cf. *Mt* 19:6-9). When man and woman have become one flesh, all the father's and mother's wounds and neglect have an impact on the living flesh of their children.

It is true, on the other hand, that there are cases in which separation is inevitable. At times it becomes even morally necessary, precisely when it is a matter of removing the weaker spouse or young children from the gravest wounds caused by abuse and violence, by humiliation and exploitation, by disregard and indifference.

There are, thanks be to God, those who, sustained by faith and by love for their children, bear witness to their fidelity to a bond they believed in, although it may seem impossible to revive it. Not all those who are separated feel called to this vocation. Not all discern, in their solitude, the Lord calling them. Around us we find various families in so-called irregular situations - I don't really like this word - and it causes us to wonder. How do we help them? How do we accompany them? How do we accompany them so that the children aren't taken hostage by either dad or mum?

Let us ask the Lord for great faith, in order to see reality through the eyes of God; and for great charity in order to approach people with his merciful heart.

FAILURE OF THE MATRIMONIAL BOND

With this catechesis we return to our reflection on the family. After speaking the last time about families wounded due to misunderstandings between spouses, today I would like to focus our attention on another reality: how to take care of those who, after an irreversible failure of their matrimonial bond, have entered into a new union.

The Church is fully aware that such a situation is contrary to the Christian Sacrament. However, her gaze as a teacher always draws from a mother's heart; a heart which, enlivened by the Holy Spirit, always seeks the good and the salvation of the people. This is why she feels obliged, "for the sake of truth", to "exercise careful discernment of situations". This is how St John Paul II expressed it in the Apostolic Exhortation *Familiaris Consortio* (n. 84), giving as an example the difference between one subjected to separation compared to one who has caused it. This discernment has to be made.

If we then also look at these new bonds through the eyes of the young sons and daughters - and the little ones watch - through the eyes of the children, we are aware of a greater urgency to foster a true welcome for these families in our communities. For this reason it is important that the style of the community, its language, its attitudes, always be attentive to people, starting with the little ones. They are the ones who suffer the most in these situations. After all, how can we encourage these parents to do everything possible to raise their children in the Christian life, to give them an example of committed and exercised faith, if we keep them at arm's length from the life of the community, as if they are excommunicated? We must act in a way so as not to add even more to the burdens which the children in these situations already feel they have to bear! Unfortunately, the number of these children and youth is really large. It is important for them to feel the Church as loving mother to all, always ready to listen and to meet.

No closed doors!

In these decades, in truth, the Church has been neither insensitive nor lazy. Thanks to the in-depth analysis performed by pastors, led and guided by my predecessors, the awareness has truly grown that it is necessary to have a fraternal and attentive welcome, in love and in truth, of the baptised who have established a new relationship of cohabitation after the failure of the marital Sacrament; in fact, these persons are by no means excommunicated - they are not excommunicated! - and they should absolutely not be treated as such: they are still a part of the Church.

Pope Benedict XVI spoke about this question, calling for careful discernment and wise pastoral accompaniment, knowing that there are no "simple solutions" ("Speech at the Seventh World Meeting of Families", Milan, 2nd June 2012, answer n. 5). Here the repeated call to pastors to openly and consistently demonstrate the community's willingness to welcome them and encourage them, so they may increasingly live and develop their membership in Christ and in the Church through prayer, by listening to the Word of God, by attending the liturgy, through the Christian education of their children, through charity and service to the poor, through the commitment to justice and peace.

The biblical icon of the Good Shepherd (*Jn* 10:11-18) summarises the mission that Jesus received from the Father: that of giving his life for the sheep. This attitude is also a model for the Church, which embraces her children as a mother who gives her life for them. "The Church is called to be the house of the Father, with doors always wide open".... No closed doors! No closed doors! "Everyone can share in some way in the life of the Church; everyone can be part of the community".... The Church "is the house of the Father, where there is a place for everyone, with all their problems" (*Evangelii Gaudium*, n. 47).

In the same way all Christians are called to imitate the Good Shepherd. Especially Christian families can co-operate with Him by taking care of wounded families, accompanying them in the life of faith of the community. Each one must play his part in taking on the attitude of the Good Shepherd, who knows each one of his sheep and excludes no one from his infinite love!

CELEBRATION

Here we open a short series of reflections on the three dimensions that articulate, so to speak, the rhythm of family life: celebration, work, prayer.

Let's begin with celebration. Today we will speak about celebration. And let's say straight away that celebration is the invention of God. Let us recall the conclusion of the story of Creation in the Book of Genesis, which we have heard:

> "And on the seventh day God finished his work which he had done, and he rested on the seventh day from all his work which he had done. So God blessed the seventh day and hallowed it, because on it God rested from all his work which he had done in creation" (2:2-3).

God himself teaches us the importance of dedicating time to contemplate and enjoy what has been done well in work. I speak of work, naturally, not only in the sense of employment and profession, but in the broader sense: every action by which we as men and women co-operate in God's creative work.

Thus celebration is not lazily lounging in an armchair, or the euphoria of foolish escape. No, celebration is first and foremost a loving and grateful look at work well done;

we celebrate work. You too, newlyweds, are celebrating the work of a fine period of engagement: and this is beautiful! It is the time to look at your children, or grandchildren, who are growing up, and to think: how beautiful! It's the time to look at our home, the friends we host, the community that surrounds us, and to think: what a good thing! God did this when he created the world. And he does so again and again, because God is always creating, even at this moment!

It is important to celebrate

It may happen that a celebration occurs in difficult or sorrowful circumstances, and perhaps we celebrate "with a lump in our throat". Yet, even in these cases, we ask God for the strength not to empty it completely. You mothers and fathers really understand this: how many times, for love of your children, you are able to swallow your sorrows so as to let them enjoy the celebration, to savour the good taste of life! There is so much love in this!

In the workplace too, at times - without neglecting our duties - we are able to let "infiltrate" a glint of celebration: a birthday, a wedding, a birth, just as a farewell or a new arrival…, it's important. It's important to celebrate. These are family moments in the inner workings of the productive machinery: it does us good!

A true moment of celebration brings work to a pause, and it is sacred, because it reminds men and women that they are made in the image of God, who is not a slave to work, but its Lord, and thus we too must never be slaves to work, but its "lords". There is a commandment about this, a commandment which concerns everyone, without exception! Yet we know that there are millions of men and women and even children who are slaves to labour! At this time there are slaves, they are exploited, slaves to labour and this is against God and against the dignity of the human person! The obsession with economic profit and technical hyper-efficiency put the human rhythms of life at risk, for life has its human rhythms. The time for rest, especially on Sunday, is ordained for us so that we can enjoy what is not produced and not consumed, not bought and not sold. Instead we see that the ideology of profit and consumerism even wants to feed on celebration: it too is sometimes reduced to a "business", to a way of making and spending money. But is this what we are working for? The greed of consumerism, which leads to waste, is an ugly virus which, among other things, makes us end up even more tired than before. It harms true labour and consumes life. Irregular rhythms of celebration often make victims of the young.

God is there in a special way

Ultimately, the time for celebration is sacred because God is there in a special way. Sunday Eucharist brings to the celebration every grace of Jesus Christ: his presence, his love, his sacrifice, his forming us into a community, his being with us…. And like this every reality receives its full meaning: work, family, the joys and trials of each day, even suffering and death; everything becomes transfigured by the grace of Christ.

The family is endowed with an extraordinary ability to understand, guide and sustain the authentic value of the time for celebration. How beautiful family celebrations are, they are beautiful! Sunday celebrations in particular. It is surely no coincidence that celebrations which have room for the whole family are those that turn out the best!

Family life itself, regarded through the eyes of faith, looks better to us than the toils that cost us. It looks to us like a masterpiece of simplicity, beautiful precisely because it is not artificial, not false, but able to incorporate within itself all aspects of real life. It looks to us like something "very good", as God says at the completion of the creation of man and woman (cf. *Gn* 1:31). Thus, celebration is a precious gift of God; a precious gift that God gave to the human family: let's not spoil it!

WORK

After having reflected on celebration in the life of the family, today we will ponder a complementary element, that of work. Both are part of God's creative design, celebration and work.

Work, as it is commonly said, is necessary for maintaining the family, for raising children, for ensuring a dignified life for our loved ones. In speaking about a serious, honest person, the most beautiful thing that can be said is: "he or she is a worker", one who works, one who in a community doesn't just live off others. There are many Argentinians today, I see, and I will say what we say: "No vive de arriba" [Don't just live it up].

And indeed work, in its many forms, beginning with that in the home, is also concerned with the common good. Where does one learn this hard working lifestyle? First of all, one learns it in the family. The family teaches work through the example of the parents: the father and the mother who work for the good of the family and of society.

In the Gospel, the Holy Family of Nazareth appears as a family of workers, and Jesus himself is called "son of a carpenter" (*Mt* 13:55) and even "the carpenter" (*Mk* 6:3). And St Paul would not fail to warn Christians: "If anyone will not work, let him not eat" (2 *Th* 3:10) - that's a good recipe for losing weight: you don't work, you don't eat! The Apostle explicitly refers to the false spiritualism of some who indeed live off their brothers and sisters "not doing any work" (2 *Th* 3:11). Commitment to work and the spiritual life, in the Christian conception, are not at all at odds with one another. It is important to understand this properly! Prayer and work can and must be in harmony, as St Benedict teaches. The absence of work damages the spirit, just as the absence of prayer damages practical activity.

Dignity of work

Work - I repeat, in its many forms - is proper to the human person. It expresses the dignity of being created in the image of God. Thus, it is said that work is sacred. And thus, managing one's occupation is a great human and social responsibility, which cannot be left in the hands of the few or unladen onto some divinised "market". Causing the loss of jobs means causing serious harm to society. It makes me sad to see people without work, who don't find work and don't have the dignity of bringing bread home. And I rejoice greatly when I see governments go to great lengths to find jobs and try to see to it that everyone has work. Work is sacred, work gives dignity to a family. We have to pray that no family is left without work.

Therefore, work too, like celebration, is part of God's creative plan. In the Book of Genesis, the theme of the earth like a back yard, entrusted to the care and cultivation of man (2, 8;15), is anticipated by a very moving passage:

> "In the day that the Lord God made the earth and the heavens, when no plant of the field was yet in the earth and no herb of the field had yet sprung up - for the Lord God had not caused it to rain upon the earth, and there was no man to till the ground; but a mist went up from the earth and watered the whole face of the ground" (2:4-6).

It's not romanticism, it is God's revelation; and we are responsible for understanding and implementing it. The Encyclical *Laudato Si'*, which proposes an integral ecology, also contains this message: the beauty of the earth and the dignity of work were made to be united. The two go together: the earth becomes beautiful when it is worked by man. When work is detached from God's covenant with man and woman, and it is separated from its spiritual qualities, when work is held hostage by the logic of profit alone and human life is disregarded, the degradation of the soul contaminates everything: even the air, water, grass, food... the life of society is corrupted and the habitat breaks down. And the consequences fall most of all on the poor and on poor families. The modern organisation of work sometimes shows a dangerous tendency to consider the family a burden, a weight, a liability for the productivity of labour. But let us ask ourselves: what productivity? And for whom? The so-called "smart city" is undoubtedly rich in services and organisation; but, for example, it is often hostile to children and the elderly. At times those in charge are interested in managing individuals as a workforce, assembling and utilising them or throwing them away on the basis of economic benefit. The family is a great workbench. When the organisation of work holds it hostage, or even blocks its path, then we can be certain that human society has begun to work against itself!

Faith and shrewdness

In this circumstance, Christian families are posed a great challenge and a great mission. They bring to the field the foundations of God's creation: the identity is the bond between man and woman, the procreation of children, the work which harnesses the earth and renders the world habitable. The loss of these foundations is a very serious matter and there are already too many cracks in the common home! It is not an easy task. Sometimes it may seem to family associations as though they are like David facing Goliath…but we know how that challenge turned out! It takes faith and shrewdness. In this difficult moment of our history, may God grant us the ability to accept with joy and hope his call, the call to work to give dignity to ourselves and to our families.

PRAYER

After reflecting on how the family lives the time of
celebration and that of work, let us now consider *the time
of prayer*. The most frequent complaint of Christians is
actually with regard to time: "I should pray more…I would
like to, but often I have no time." We hear it all the time.
The regret is sincere, certainly, because the human heart
always desires prayer, even without realising it; and if it
doesn't find it, it is not at peace. But in order to find it, we
need to cultivate in our hearts an "ardent" love for God, an
affectionate love.

Let us ask a very simple question. It's good to believe in
God with all our heart, it's good to hope that he will help
us in difficulty, it's good to feel obliged to give him thanks.
All this is just; but *do we love the Lord, even a little*? Does
the thought of God move us, amaze us, soften us?

Let us think of the wording of that great Commandment,
which is the basis of all others: "you shall love the Lord your
God with all your heart, and with all your soul, and with
all your might" (*Dt* 6:5; cf. *Mt* 22:37). The formula uses
the intense language of love, addressing it to God. See, the
spirit of prayer dwells here above all. And if it dwells here, *it
dwells all the time* and never leaves. Are we able to think of

God as the caress that keeps us alive, before which there is nothing? A caress from which nothing, not even death, can separate us? Or do we think of him only as the Great Being, the Almighty who made all things, the Judge who monitors every action? All true, of course; but only when God is the affection above all our affections, does the meaning of these words find their fullness. Then we feel happy, even if a little confused, because he thinks of us and above all he loves us! Isn't that impressive? Isn't it impressive that God caresses us with the love of a father? It is so beautiful! He could have simply revealed himself as the Supreme Being, given his commandments and waited for the results. Instead, God did and does infinitely more than this. He accompanies us on life's journey, he protects us, he loves us.

Time for prayer

If love for God does not light the fire, the spirit of prayer will not warm time. We may also multiply our words, "as the pagans do", says Jesus; or even perform our rituals, "as the Pharisees do" (cf. *Mt* 6:5,7). A heart which is home to affection for God makes a prayer of an unspoken thought, or an invocation before a holy image, or a kiss blown to the Church. It's beautiful when mothers teach their little children to blow kisses to Jesus or to Our Lady. What tenderness there is in this! In that moment the child's heart is transformed into a place of prayer. And it is a gift of the Holy Spirit. Let us never forget to ask for this gift for each one of us! Because the Spirit of God has that special way of saying in our heart "Abba" - "Father". It teaches us to say "Father" just as Jesus said it, a way that we can never find on our own (cf. *Ga* 4:6). *It is in the family that one learns to ask for and appreciate this gift of the Spirit.* If one learns to say it with the same spontaneity with which one learns "father" and "mother," one has learned it forever. When this happens, the time of the whole of family life is enveloped in the womb of God's love, and seeks spontaneously the time of prayer.

We know well that family time is a complicated and crowded time, busy and preoccupied. There is always little, there is never enough, there are so many things to do. One who has a family soon learns to solve an equation that not even the great mathematicians know how to solve: within twenty four hours they make twice that many! There are mothers and fathers who could win the Nobel Prize for this. Out of twenty four hours they make forty eight: I don't know how they do it, but they get on and do it! There is so much work in a family!

Give time back to God

The spirit of prayer gives time back to God, it steps away from the obsession of a life that is always lacking time, it rediscovers the peace of necessary things and discovers the joy of unexpected gifts. Two good guides for this are the sisters Martha and Mary, spoken of in the Gospel we have just heard; they learned from God the harmony of family rhythms: the beauty of celebration, the serenity of work, the spirit of prayer (cf. *Lk* 10:38-42). The visit of Jesus, whom they loved, was their celebration. However, one day Martha learned that the work of hospitality, though important, is not everything, but that listening to the Lord, as Mary did, was the really essential thing, the "best kind" of time. Prayer flows from listening to Jesus, from reading the Gospel. Do not forget to read a passage of the Gospel every day. Prayer flows from closeness to the Word of God. Is there this closeness in our family? Do we have the Gospel at home? Do we open it sometimes to read it together? Do we meditate on it while reciting the Rosary? The Gospel read and meditated on as a family is like good bread that nourishes everyone's heart. In the morning and in the evening, and when we sit at the table, we learn to say together a prayer with great simplicity: it is Jesus who comes among us, as he was with the family of Martha, Mary and Lazarus. There is something that is very close to my heart; because I have seen it in the city: there are children who have not learned to make the Sign of the Cross! But you, mother, father, teach your child to pray, to make the Sign of the Cross: this is a lovely task for mothers and fathers!

In the prayer of the family, in its intense moments and in its difficult seasons, we are entrusted to one another, so that each one of us in the family may be protected by the love of God.

EVANGELISATION

In this last stage on our journey of catecheses on the family, let us broaden our gaze to the way in which it lives out its responsibility to *communicate the faith*, to transmit the faith, both inside and out.

At first, what may come to mind are several Gospel expressions that seem to oppose the bonds of family and the following of Christ. For example, the strong words that we all know and we all have heard: "He who loves father or mother more than me is not worthy of me; and he who loves son or daughter more than me is not worthy of me" (*Mt* 10:37-38).

Naturally, by this Jesus doesn't intend to cancel out the fourth Commandment, which importantly is the first Commandment directed at others. The first three are in relation to God, this one is directed at people. Nor can we think that, after performing his miracle for the newlyweds in Cana, after consecrating the marriage bond between man and woman, after restoring sons and daughters to the life of the family, would the Lord ask us to be insensitive to these bonds! This is not the explanation. On the contrary, when Jesus affirms the primacy of faith in God, he finds no paragon more fitting than that of familial love. Moreover, these same familial bonds, within the experience of the faith and love of God, are transformed, they become "filled" with greater meaning and become capable of *going beyond themselves*, to create a fatherhood and motherhood, and to welcome as brothers and sisters also those who are on the margins of every familial bond. One day, to those who told him that his mother and brothers were outside looking for him, Jesus responds, pointing to his disciples: "Here are my mother and my brothers! Whoever does the will of God is my brother, and sister, and mother" (*Mk* 3:34-35).

Familial affections

Emotional maturity can't be bought or sold and it is the greatest endowment of the familial genius. It is precisely in the family where we learn to grow in the atmosphere of emotional maturity. Its "grammar" is learned there, otherwise it is very difficult to learn it. And it is through this language that God makes us all understand.

The invitation to place family ties within the context of obedience to the faith and to the covenant with the Lord does not demean them; on the contrary it protects them, frees them from selfishness, protects them from degradation, rescues them for life which knows no death. A familial style that flows through human relationships *is a blessing for the peoples*: it brings hope back to the land. When familial affections are allowed to convert to the Gospel witness, they become capable of inconceivable things, which make tangible the works of God, those works which God performs in history, such as those which Jesus did for the men, women and children he encountered. Just one smile miraculously rising out of the desperation of an abandoned child, who is beginning to live again, explains God's action in the world better than a thousand theological treatises. One man and one woman, capable of risking and sacrificing themselves for another's child and not just for their own, explains the matters of love better than any scientist. And wherever there are such familial affections, there too arise these heartfelt gestures that are more eloquent than words. The gesture of love.... This makes us think.

Ferment like the leaven of God

The family that responds to the call of Jesus *consigns the stewardship of the world back to the covenant of man and woman with God*. Imagine developing this testimony today. Let us imagine that the headline of the story (of society, of the economy, of politics) is relegated - finally! - to the covenant of man and woman, in order that they tend to it with their gaze directed at the generations to come. The themes of earth and home, of the economy and of work, would sing a very different tune!

If we were - beginning with the Church - to centre our attention on the family that listens and practises the Word of God, we would become like the good wine of the wedding feast of Cana, we would ferment like the leaven of God!

Indeed, the family's covenant with God is called today to counteract the community desertification of the modern city. But the lack of love and smiling has turned our cities into deserts. So much entertainment, so many things for wasting time, for making laughter, but love is lacking. The smile of a family can overcome this desertification of our cities. This is the victory of family love. No economic and political engineering can substitute this contribution of families. The Babel project builds lifeless skyscrapers. The Spirit of God instead makes the desert fruitful (cf. *Is* 32:15). We must come out of the towers and from the armoured vaults of the elite, to again spend time in the homes and open spaces of the multitudes, open to the love of families.

The communion of charisms - those bestowed in the Sacrament of Marriage and those granted at consecration through the Kingdom of God - is intended to transform the Church into a fully familial place through the encounter with God. Let us go forth on this path, let us not lose hope. Wherever there is a loving family, that family with its witness of love is capable of warming the heart of an entire city.

Pray for me, let us pray for one another, that we become capable of recognising and supporting the visits of God. The Spirit will bring happy disarray to Christian families, and the city of man will rise from its depression.

COMMUNITY

I would like to focus our attention on the connection between the family and the Christian community. This bond is natural, so to speak, because the Church is a spiritual family and the family is the domestic Church (cf. *Lumen Gentium*, n. 9, 11).

The Christian community is the home of those who believe in Jesus as the font of brotherhood among all human beings. The Church journeys among her people, in the history of men and women, of fathers and mothers, of sons and daughters: this is the history that matters to the Lord. The great events of worldly powers are written in history books, and there they will remain. But the history of human feelings is written directly in the heart of God; and that is the history that will endure for eternity. This is where life and faith are located. The family is the place of our irreplaceable and indelible initiation into this history…into this history of life in its fullness, which will culminate in heaven with the contemplation of God for all eternity, but which begins in the family! And that is why the family is so important.

The Son of God learned the human story in this way, and he walked in it to the very end (cf. *Heb* 2:18; 5:8). It is beautiful to contemplate Jesus and the signs of this bond! He was born into a family and there "he learned about the world": one shop, four homes or so, a tiny village. Yet, living for thirty years there, Jesus absorbed the human condition, welcoming it in his communion with the Father and in his apostolic mission. Then, when he left Nazareth and began his public ministry, Jesus formed around him a community, an "assembly", that is, a convocation of people. This is the meaning of the word "church".

This family of God's guests

In the Gospels, the assembly of Jesus takes the form of a family and of a hospitable family, not an exclusive, closed sect: there we find Peter and John, but also the hungry and the thirsty, the stranger and the persecuted, the sinner and the tax collector, the Pharisee and the multitude. And Jesus never stops accepting and speaking to everyone, even those who no longer expect to encounter God in this life. That is an important lesson for the Church! The disciples were chosen to care for this assembly, for this family of God's guests.

In order to maintain this reality of the assembly of Jesus in today's situation, it is indispensable to renew the covenant between the family and the Christian community. We could say that the family and the parish are the two places where the communion of love, which finds its ultimate source in God, takes place. A Church truly according to the Gospel cannot but take the form of a hospitable home, with its doors open, always. Churches, parishes, institutions with closed doors must never be called churches, they should be called museums!

And today, this covenant is crucial. "Against the ideological, financial and political 'centres of power', we place our hopes in these centres of evangelizing love, rich in human warmth, based on solidarity and participation" (Pontifical Council for the Family, *The Teachings of J.M. Bergoglio-Pope Francis on the Family and Life 1999-2014*, LEV 2014, 189), and also on forgiveness among us.

Family and community bonds

Strengthening the bond between the family and the Christian community today is indispensable and urgent. Certainly, there is need for generous faith in order to rediscover the understanding and courage to renew this covenant. Families at times draw back, saying that they cannot live up to this: "Father, we are a poor family and even a little worse for the wear", "We aren't able", "We already have so many problems at home", "We don't have the strength." This is true. But no one is worthy, no one is able to live up to it, no one has the strength! Without the grace of God, we can do nothing. Everything is given to us, given freely! And the Lord never comes into a new family without working some miracle. Let us remember what he did at the wedding at Cana! Yes, if we place ourselves in his hands, the Lord will work miracles for us - but they are miracles of everyday life! - when the Lord is there, present in the family.

Naturally, the Christian community must also play its part. For example, overcoming attitudes that give too much advice or are too managerial, in order to foster interpersonal dialogue and awareness and mutual esteem. May families take the initiative and feel the responsibility for bringing their precious gifts to the community. We must all be aware that the Christian faith is played on an open field of life shared with all. The family and the parish must work the miracle of a more communal life for the whole of society.

At Cana, there was the Mother of Jesus, the "mother of good counsel". Let us listen to her words: "Do whatever he tells you" (cf. *Jn* 2:5). Dear families, dear parish communities, let us allow ourselves to be inspired by this Mother, let us do whatever Jesus tells us and we will find the source of all miracles, of everyday miracles!

NATIONS

The current transition in civilisation seems to be marked by the long-lasting effects of a society governed by economic technocracy. This subordination of ethics to the logic of profit commands substantial resources and the widespread support of the media. In this context, a new covenant between man and woman has become not only necessary, but crucial for emancipating humanity from the colonisation of money. This covenant should once again guide politics, the economy and civil co-existence! It decides the habitability of the earth, the transmission of love for life, the bonds of memory and hope.

In this covenant, the familial-conjugal union of man and woman is the generative grammar, the "golden knot", we might say. The faith draws it from the wisdom of the creation of God, who has entrusted to the family, not the care of intimacy as an end in itself, but rather the exciting project of making the world "domestic". At the beginning there was the family, at the root of this world culture that saves us...saves us from many, many attacks, from so much destruction, from so many "colonisations", like that of money or of the ideologies that threaten so much of the world. The family is the basis of our defence!

We have taken our essential inspiration for these brief Wednesday reflections on the family from the biblical Word of creation. From this Word we can and we must once again draw anew abundantly and deeply. A great and very exciting undertaking awaits us. God's creation is not a mere philosophical premise: it is the universal horizon of life and of faith! There is no divine plan other than creation and its salvation. It is for the salvation of creatures - of every creature - that God became man: "for us men and for our salvation", as the Creed says. And the Risen Jesus is "the first-born of all creation" (*Col* 1:15).

The created world was entrusted to man and to woman: what takes place between them marks everything. Their rejection of God's blessing fatally leads them to a delirium of omnipotence that ruins everything. That is what we call "original sin". And we all bear the inheritance of this disease from birth.

God's merciful protection

Nevertheless, we are not cursed, nor are we abandoned to ourselves. The ancient account of God's first love for man and woman already had fire written into its pages in this regard! "I will put enmity between you and the woman, and between your seed and her seed" (*Gn* 3:15a). These are the words God directs to the serpent deceiver, the serpent charmer! Through these words God marks woman with a protective barrier against evil, to which she can turn - if she wants - in every generation. It means that woman carries within her a secret and a special blessing, to defend his creation from the evil one! Like the woman in the Book of Revelation, who hastens to hide the child from the dragon. And God shields her (cf. *Rv* 12:6).

Think what depth is opened here! There exist many stereotypes, some rather offensive, about the woman temptress who inspires evil. On the contrary, there is room for a theology of woman worthy of this blessing of God for her and for every generation!

The merciful protection of God for man and woman, in every case, never fails either of them. Let us not forget this! The symbolic language of the Bible tells us that before exiling them from the Garden of Eden, God made for man and woman garments of skins, and clothed them (cf. *Gn* 3:21). This act of tenderness means that in the painful consequences of our sin, God does not want us to be left naked and abandoned to our fate as sinners.

This divine tenderness, this care for us, we see incarnated in Jesus of Nazareth, Son of God "born of woman" (*Ga* 4:4). And St Paul says ever and again: "while we were yet sinners Christ died for us" (*Rm* 5:8). Christ, born of woman, of a woman. That is God's gentle caress upon our wounds, upon our errors, upon our sins. God loves us as we are and desires to lead us forward in this plan, and woman is the stronger one who carries this plan forward.

The promise God makes to man and woman, at the start of history, extends to all human beings, until the end of time. If we have enough faith, the families of the all the nations of the earth will recognise themselves in this blessing. In every way, anyone who feels moved by this vision, whatever people, nation or religion to which they may belong, let them take up the journey with us. He and she will be our brother and sister, without having to proselytise them. Let us walk together in this blessing and in the plan of God to make us all brothers and sisters in the life of a world which moves forward and which is born from the family, from the union of man and woman.

May God bless you, families from every corner of the earth! May God bless you all!

Sources

This booklet draws together the catecheses given at General Audiences by Pope Francis which took place in Rome between 17th December 2014 and 16th September 2015.

Nazareth: Pope Francis, General Audience, 17th December 2014.
The Mother: Pope Francis, General Audience, 7th January 2015.
The Absent Father: Pope Francis, General Audience, 28th January 2015.
The Father who is Present: Pope Francis, General Audience, 4th February 2015.
The Children: Pope Francis, General Audience, 11th February 2015.
Brothers and Sisters: Pope Francis, General Audience, 18th February 2015.
The Elderly: Pope Francis, General Audience, 4th March 2015.
The Grandparents: Pope Francis, General Audience, 11th March 2015.
The Gift of Children: Pope Francis, General Audience, 18th March 2015.
The Sufferings of Children: Pope Francis, General Audience, 8th April 2015.
The Creation of Man and Woman: Pope Francis, General Audience, 15th April 2015.
In His Own Image: Pope Francis, General Audience, 22nd April 2015.
Marriage: Pope Francis, General Audience, 29th April 2015.
The Beauty of Christian Marriage: Pope Francis, General Audience, 6th May 2015.
The Three Expressions: Pope Francis, General Audience, 13th May 2015.
Education: Pope Francis, General Audience, 20th May 2015.
Engagement: Pope Francis, General Audience, 27th May 2015.
Family and Poverty: Pope Francis, General Audience, 3rd June 2015.
Family and Illness: Pope Francis, General Audience, 10th June 2015.
Death: Pope Francis, General Audience, 17th June 2015.
Wounds: Pope Francis, General Audience, 24th June 2015.
Failure of the Matrimonial Bond: Pope Francis, General Audience, 5th August 2015.
Celebration: Pope Francis, General Audience, 12th August 2015. Work: Pope Francis, General Audience, 19th August 2015.
Prayer: Pope Francis, General Audience, 26th August 2015.
Evangelisation: Pope Francis, General Audience, 2nd September 2015.
Community: Pope Francis, General Audience, 9th September 2015.
Nations: Pope Francis, General Audience, 16th September 2015.